Reading Revelation in Babylon

Actualizing the Apocalypse

By Canaan Harris

EPANGELIA

Cover image:
Wassily Kandinsky, *The Last Judgment*, 1912,
Private collection, Munich, Germany.

ISBN: 978-1-953336-01-9 (paperback)
ISBN: 978-1-953336-12-5 (hardback)
ISBN: 978-1-953336-05-7 (digital)

Epangelia Press
3690 Cherry Creek South Drive
Denver, CO 80033
www.epangeliapress.com

"If our love were but more faithful,
we would take God at His word."

There's A Wideness in God's Mercy,
Frederick Faber, 1859

Contents

Prologue

Written in 2007 as a graduate thesis for Yale Divinity School, this book represents my first attempt to interpret the Book of Revelation for a contemporary audience. Originally titled *Apocalyptic Ethics: Reading Revelation in Babylon*, it began as a synthesis between my graduate work in Christian ethics under Margaret Farley and my studies in New Testament exegesis under Adela Yarbro Collins. My task was to show how Revelation can be read in every generation, including ours, as a "parable" that teaches us how to live in anticipation of Christ's return.

Later that same year, I put aside my academic studies when I accepted the call to be a church pastor in Denver, Colorado. Then in 2010, in an effort to teach Revelation in the church, I dug out my old thesis again and fluffed it, abbreviating some of the more scholarly portions in order to make it more accessible for the layperson. This reconditioned version - called *Reading Revelation in Babylon* - is the same book I am publishing today. Back then I printed a very small run on a copy machine and spiral-bound them at Kinkos to share with a few friends. Otherwise I pretty much kept the book to myself, using it as an organizational method and as reference material to teach two popular Bible studies on Revelation in the church, not to mention numerous sermon series and lectures over the past ten years.

As a result of this work, the Book of Revelation has become not only the primary lens by which I read the events of the news but it is also my instruction book for how to live out my role as a "stranger and sojourner" in this world (1 Pet. 2:11). Yet because the subject matter is so provocative, to date the book has remained unpublished and unappreciated outside of my small circle of friends and my local congregation. For as a Christian minister ordained in a mainline denominational church, I have no illusions as to the skepticism with which 99.9% of my colleagues consider these ideas. Plus, as the pastor of an established local congregation with a lot of church politics to contend with (not to mention my role as a husband and a father) I have plenty of other responsibilities on my plate.

Nevertheless, I have continued to watch and to wait for signs of the times. For while this book argues that Revelation can be read as a parable to describe the role of the church in any era, it still anticipates a final Apocalypse and according to my calculations it appears we may be nearing the End Times of prophecy. This timetable, even as it is now coinciding with current events, has finally persuaded me that it is time to share this message so it can become a resource for anyone who is interested in actualizing the Book of Revelation.

Another reason I am now releasing this book in its original form is because so many friends have asked me privately to comment on events in the news that I plan to write a new book to speak specifically to the modern-day context. Written in the style of a memoir, my new book will reflect so directly on the material in the old one that initially I just planned to update the original manuscript. Yet so much has happened over the past 14 years that it seems many of the questions I raised in the 2007 book may have already been answered, while most of the actualizing references are now long out-of-date. So after a few feeble attempts at revising it, I thought it better just to publish the 2007 book again retroactively, with all the references intact and without any revision, so that I can then refer back to it in the next book - coming soon!

For without Revelation, the church has no template by which to understand our role relative to nation-states and governments. Without Revelation, Christians could just claim ignorance of the very real and present danger of pledging allegiance to idolatrous authorities ... that is, until it is too late. Revelation is thus unapologetically a political book, questioning the world's narrative of the contest between church and state and providing a counter-narrative in the same way it did for the people of ancient Rome, etceteras. Unfortunately, if we fail to read and interpret Revelation, as many Christians do, we will fail to recognize the proper role of Christians in relation to the contemporary Babylon system of our day.

Indeed, Revelation contains specific instruction on how Christians must comport ourselves in relation to the government authorities in every generation. For the danger of Christians forgetting our proper role relative to these political realities is the danger of falling victim to totalitarianism, or even of the church becoming the very handmaiden of empire. Thus as Christians living in a time in which "the powers of this dark world" (Eph. 6:12) have effected a system of total full-spectrum dominance over human lives to a degree never before seen in history, we cannot forget to heed the prophecy of John's Apocalypse.

Canaan Harris
March 26, 2021

Why Read Revelation?

*This is the awful truth that we have yet to recognize.
We are living in an apocalyptic time disguised as
normal, and that is why we have not responded
appropriately.* – Walter Wink[1]

F rom the Greek Ἀποκάλυψις, meaning "to
reveal or unveil," the Apocalypse to John
envisions an epic battle between the hosts
of heaven and the evil kingdoms of this world in
which Jesus will return to confront the Antichrist

---

[1] See Walter Wink, "Apocalypse Now?" *The Christian
Century*, Oct. 17, 2001, 16-19.

11

and judge the living and the dead.[2] For those with eyes to see and ears to hear, it may appear that even now the stage is being set for these events surrounding the end of time. "About that day or hour no one knows" (Mk. 13:32), but Revelation's prophecy instructs us to keep watch for signs of the end times that we might not be found asleep at Christ's return.

Traditionally, Christians are to be ever on the alert for Christ's return, and a reading of Revelation in light of present-day circumstances indicates to this interpreter that the time may be at hand. To those who choose to interpret Revelation as a prophetic word or as a parable for our time, it may appear that certain spiritual realities are presently unfolding which indicate that Revelation's prophecy will soon be fulfilled, perhaps even in this generation.

---

[2] The word *apocalypse* means to reveal or unveil a truth hidden from plain view; accordingly, John's apocalypse is concerned with the "revelation" of Jesus as promised Messiah. Apocalypse is also the literary genre of Revelation, as stated in the title: "The Revelation [Ἀποκάλυψις] of Jesus Christ" (Rev.1:1).

The Time is Near

While no biblical interpretation is infallible, if this prediction is correct it means that life as we know it will change dramatically. Revelation predicts that Christian people will undergo a terrible season of persecution but will ultimately survive the climactic battle of Armageddon. This is good news in that, in the end, Christ will return in triumph, evil will be vindicated, the earth will be renewed, and those who remain faithful will enter into everlasting life.

To the secular mind it might seem a paradox, but the Apocalypse will be a happy event for people of faith.

To the secular mind it might seem a paradox, but in this way the Apocalypse will be a happy event for people of faith. "Happy is he who reads aloud the words of this prophecy," writes John, "and happy are those who hear and who keep what is written in it, for the time is near" (Rev. 1:3).

A call to have faith in God rather than empire, Revelation is a pertinent witness for these times, a guide for those who live in exile in what some call "our American Babylon."[3] Thus Revelation can be particularly helpful to modern-day Christians in that it was written as a manual for a church in conflict with political authorities in both the temporal and spiritual realms.

What it teaches us is how we are to relate to the power of governments and nations and empires as strangers and sojourners, or resident aliens: with primary citizenship, not in any state or nation, but in Christ's church. This teaching alone constitutes mandatory instruction for Christians living in relation to any political authority, in any time or place, for it tells us how to comport ourselves in relation to competing claims on our political allegiance. Consequently, it really doesn't matter whether the end is coming in our era or in some time unforeseen, for we are called to behave as citizens of Christ's church in all times and places.

---

[3] "America is not uniquely Babylon," claims Richard Neuhaus, "but it is our time and place in Babylon." Richard John Neuhaus, "Our American Babylon," *First Things* 158, Dec. 2005, 23-28.

In this way, Christians today are no different than those of generations before, in that we must inevitably live as resident aliens or "strangers in a strange land" in relation to any political authority. Already we are hard-pressed to preserve our Christian faith and values in the face of a widening cultural morass. However, in recent years it has become evident that certain advances in technology hold potential to facilitate an advance in political and intellectual totalitarianism in which human beings will be atomized – divided from our natural allegiances within the human family and re-oriented toward service to the state – like never before in human history.

As a Christian living in contention with the Roman Empire, John the Revelator saw this atomization beginning to transpire in his time, and God gave him this prophecy of Revelation in order to instruct Christians on how to maintain our faith in the face of empire and its absolute claims. Having had this vision, John naturally described it in terms of his own experience in relation to the Roman Empire. The parable of Revelation, however, has since been read and understood in every epoch as instruction for Christians on how to live in relation to the claims of church and state.

Revelation has been instructive, even essential, to Christians persecuted under the Spanish Inquisition, for example, or in Nazi death camps or Soviet gulags. And in much the same way, Revelation can be instructive to Christians today, living under the threat of more modern cultural and political empires; and now perhaps for the first time, living under the threat of persecution by One World Government. The advancement of technology, social engineering, and global communication to the point where One World Government seems a legitimate possibility is but one reason why the prophecy of Revelation is now more important than ever.

Prophecy as Parable

Revelation can help us to understand God's plan for the future of this earth, and to recognize the evidence of this plan finally coming to pass. Recognizing the signs of Christ's return can help Christians to find hope even in the most difficult of circumstances. Revelation also alerts us to the

nature of certain realities of the spiritual realm
that will dictate the return of Christ to earth.

*Recognizing the signs of Christ's return
can help Christians to find hope even in
the most difficult of circumstances.*

Consequently, Revelation empowers Christians to
recognize when temporal realities so correspond
to these spiritual realities that God's plan will be
set in motion. Such open discussion of Christian
prophecy and apocalyptic may be unfamiliar to
many modern readers, who are often skeptical of
anything too fantastic or irrational. Yet such
teaching is nothing new, for throughout the New
Testament those who trust in God's promises are
taught to wait for the coming of the Lord.

The scripture says that, "in accordance with his
promise, we wait for a new heaven and a new
earth, where righteousness is at home" (2 Pt.
3:13). As the final book of the Bible, the prophecy
of Revelation reveals to us the end of the story,
the climax of the journey of Christian faith, or
that for which we wait. In the meantime,
Revelation remains instructive as it has for

Christians throughout history, particularly those suffering persecution.

True, we do not know the day or the hour of Christ's coming, but the parable of Revelation was given to us so that we might have some insight into God's plan for our future. For this reason, I have found it necessary to write this work of interpretation, for in my experience the church is in great need of instruction in this regard. My ecclesial perspective is from the denominational church in North America, specifically as a pastor in the Christian Church (Disciples of Christ), a liberal mainline church of declining influence on American religious life, and I recognize that this has limited my exposure to church movements that are surely more familiar with end-time prophecy. The church as I have experienced it is woefully uninformed on the subject of eschatology, to the point of dismissing it altogether.

Indeed, the church as I see it suffers a lack of purpose and identity precisely because it fails to read and interpret the book of Revelation as parable and apply it to our place and time.

Because we do not read Revelation, we fail to recognize that we must always live as strangers and aliens in relation to political authorities, and as a result we seem to constantly find ourselves in bed with one political administration or another. Because we do not read Revelation, we cannot see the spiritual realities that exist behind the temporal concerns of our churches, and thus are ill-equipped to engage these concerns with spiritual weapons and resources.

We read Revelation, then, because we want to live as the gospel commands in anticipation of Christ's return, and we want to know the end of the story. We read Revelation, also, to encourage us in our primary citizenship as members of the church of Christ, living as strangers and sojourners in regards to governments of nations. Moreover, we read Revelation as a manual for living as a church in spiritual conflict with the powers and principalities of the earth, equipping us for spiritual warfare against the forces of Satan. And we read Revelation as a parable for our time, seeking to discern the sign of Christ's coming in the news of the day.

A Manual for Living

Reading Revelation will empower Christians to find a renewed hope and purpose and position in this world, not as mere constituents of an association held under authority of earthly governments, but as part of a movement of the spirit of God that contends with spiritual powers in heavenly places, awaiting the culmination of the promise of Christ's return. We hold fast to this hope, remembering that "the Lord is not slow about his promise, as some think of slowness, but is patient with you, not wanting any to perish, but all to come to repentance" (2 Pt. 3:9).

God only knows, but it could be that mainline denominational folks like me, who represent just a tiny minority of Christians around the world, are the only ones that remain unconcerned with Revelation's prophecy, and I pray that this is true. But, at the very least, we in the mainline church are in need of a wake-up call and a reorientation to the promise of Christ's return. This book intends to do just that: to prompt the church to consider Revelation as a parable for our time. To this end what follows is a verse by verse exegesis of Revelation as it applies to modern-day concerns, with the express hope of discovering parallels between Revelation's prophecy and contemporary culture and political realities.

"The Lord is not slow about his promise but is patient with you, not wanting any to perish, but all to come to repentance" (2 Peter 3:9).

This is difficult work for many, as it presupposes that this letter is actually prophetic and revealed from God, and liberal interpreters are often uncomfortable in making these assumptions. Therefore, in an effort to circumvent skepticism, this project is governed by an interpretive principle that intends to transcend the divide between church and academy. The chapter on hermeneutics defines a strategy of interpretation called "*actualization*" whereby one can "actualize" (imagine) that any particular context is a potential setting for the apocalyptic scenario, thereby freeing the rational mind to consider the possibility that Revelation could be in any way prescient or prophetic.

For those of us accustomed to contemplating biblical prophecy this emphasis on hermeneutics or interpretive strategy might seem pedantic, yet it is quite necessary for readers who are heavily indoctrinated into the cult of reason but who still wish to gain some entry into what might at first glance seem to be an "irrational" conversation about biblical prophecy. In practical terms, this hermeneutic strategy of actualization allows the interpreter to utilize both academic and prophetic scholarship in seeking to understand the text.

Why read Revelation? It may be that the question is already answered, and if not, I pray that this line of discussion will help the reader find the answer for himself. You may find, as I do, that Revelation becomes invaluable in that it helps us recognize the powers and principalities for what they are and to find spiritual resources to contend with them. In this way, Revelation is as important to my understanding of the Christian faith as any other New Testament book, and it is my sincere hope that this work will convey such a sense of practical application to its readers.

Interpreting Revelation: A History

Every single empire, in its official discourse, has said it is not like all the others, that its circumstances are special, that it has a mission to enlighten, civilize, bring order and democracy, and that it uses force only as a last resort.
- Edward Said[4]

D ismissed by many contemporary authorities as gibberish, in truth Revelation offers a revolutionary reinterpretation of events that challenges the dominant propaganda, proposing a narrative of

---

[4] Edward Said, "Preface to Orientalism," *Al-Ahram*, Aug. 2003, 7-13.

existence that constitutes a radical alternative to the status quo. The author, John of Patmos, was thought by early theologians to be John the Apostle; however, contemporary textual criticism suggests that these were two different individuals.[5] Written from the perspective of a people oppressed by an empire that claimed ultimate authority, Revelation relates John's vision of a cosmic battle consummating in the destruction of Satan and the demonic city of Babylon, and the triumph of God's faithful in the new city of Jerusalem.

A circular pastoral letter addressed to seven churches in the imperial province of Asia at the end of the first century C.E., the Apocalypse to John was written to be read aloud in the midst of the worshipping community, so as to encourage the perseverance of early Christians threatened by Roman persecution.[6] To a contemporary

---

[5] The author is known as John of Patmos because he identifies himself as John (1:1, 4, 9; 22:8), and because he claims that he received his first vision while in exile on the island of Patmos (1:9; 4:1–2).

[6] Revelation was likely written during the reign of Domitian (81-96 CE). See Eugene Boring, *Revelation* (Louisville: John Knox Press, 1989), 8-10.

culture accustomed to chronologically based narratives Revelation can seem enigmatic: the message is given in pictorial language utilizing florid imagery in a complex numerological pattern of recapitulation replete with allusions to astrology, Roman cultic practices, popular apocalypticism, and the Hebrew prophets. Yet in the time that it was written Revelation would have been clearly understood as a polemic against the Roman Empire.

Naming Rome "Babylon" may well have kept this message secret from the Roman authorities, but to an audience intimately familiar with Jewish history it would have been obvious that Rome was the spiritual equivalent of Babylon, where the Jews were held in captivity in the time of the prophets. As Revelation was read by each successive generation of believers, "Babylon" eventually became descriptive of other political powers that have oppressed Christians throughout history.

Then as now, to name the proponents of empire "Satan" easily offends, and has made Revelation one of the most despised and controversial books of the New Testament (and consequently the subject of conflicting interpretations). Even before Revelation was written, the early church was so fervently anticipating the Second Coming of Christ that Paul found it necessary to warn Christians not to be deceived into believing that Christ had already returned.[7]

Paul taught that there first must be apostasy and the revelation of "the man of lawlessness" (2 Thessalonians 2:1-12).

A generation later, apocalypticists such as Justin Martyr and Irenaeus adopted a chiliastic (or millennial) perspective, interpreting the Apocalypse in light of Genesis' creation story and 2 Peter 3:8 to mean that the world would last 6,000 years until Jesus' return, when the church

---

[7] Paul taught that there first must be apostasy and the revelation of "the man of lawlessness" (2 Thessalonians 2:1-12). However, a few early theologians, such as Papias in the first-century, persisted in interpreting the apocalyptic tradition to mean that Christ's resurrection had already inaugurated his reign.

would reign with him a thousand years.[8] A few early theologians, such as Origen and Clement of Alexandria, argued that Revelation should be interpreted allegorically. As persecution increased at the hands of Roman authorities, however, more and more Christians expected the immanent return of Christ; Hippolytus of Rome, for example, predicted that Christ would return in the year 496.

Church and State

Everything changed after Emperor Constantine issued the Edict of Milan in 313. Legitimizing Christianity in the empire effectively ended the persecution of Christians while increasingly entangling relations between the church and the imperial state; as a result, Christian theologians soon found it advantageous to interpret scripture in a manner favorable to Rome. In the fourth century, Augustine rejected the chiliastic view of the eschaton accepted since Irenaeus in favor of

---

[8] Victorinus of Poetovio, author of the first commentary on Revelation written in 260, shared this chiliastic perspective. Victorinus' work was preserved thanks to Jerome," write Kovacs and Rowland, "who issued a revised edition of it in 398 in which the chiliastic elements were removed" (See Kovacs and Rowland, 15).

the more allegorical reading of Origen and Tyconius, a position that influenced the church for centuries.[9] Around the same time, bishops such as John Chrysostom argued against including the Apocalypse in the New Testament canon, citing the difficulty of interpreting it and the danger for abuse.

Christian interest in eschatology waned in the centuries to follow. Then, in the latter Middle Ages, the monastic reformer Joachim of Fiore (c.1135-1202) broke with the Augustinian tradition, finding in the Apocalypse the key to the bible and all of history.[10] Joachim's interpretation mirrored that of early Christianity by recognizing eschatological significance in the present time. He influenced later movements that saw

---

[9] Preserved only through the works of his contemporaries, Tyconius' lost commentary was the earliest to emphasize the dual perspective of Revelation: "[Revelation] mixes together two times," claims Tyconius, "now present, now future." Quoted in Beatus of Liebana, *Commentary on the Apocalypse*, ed. H.A. Sanders (Rome: American Academy, 1930), 12.2.1). The dominant interpretation of the 8th century, Beatus' *Commentary* circulated through the monasteries, copied out by hand for more than four centuries.

[10] See E. Rudolph Daniel, "Joachim of Fiore: Patterns of History in the Apocalypse," *The Apocalypse in the Middle Ages,* eds. Richard K. Emmerson and Bernard McGinn (Ithica, NY: Cornell University Press, 1993), 72-88.

themselves as participants in the end times, thus contributing much to the social upheavals of this era.[11]

Revelation mixes together two times - now present, now future.

At first, the Protestant Reformers had little use for Revelation. In the annotations to his Greek New Testament, Erasmus called the legitimacy of Revelation into question, and initially Martin Luther agreed, separating Revelation from the other books in his 1522 New Testament and writing that he considered Revelation to be "neither apostolic nor prophetic," stating moreover that "Christ is neither taught nor known in it."[12] Once Luther realized how helpful the Apocalypse could be for anti-Catholic polemic, however, he subtly modified his viewpoint so as to better characterize the Pope as

---

[11] See Norman Cohn, *The Pursuit of the Millennium* (London: Paladin, 1957), 205-22.

[12] Paul Althaus, *The Theology of Martin Luther* (Philadelphia: Fortress, 1966), 85.

the Antichrist.[13] In contrast, Roman Catholic interpreters like Robert Bellarmine would utilize a preterist or futurist hermeneutic in their attempts to neutralize Luther's actualizing interpretation.[14]

After the Reformation, the church splintered into hundreds of separate sects, each of which was influenced to some degree by the Apocalypse. Some interpreters, claiming divine inspiration, declared themselves to be ordained by God to establish the New Jerusalem as described in Revelation: consider the Anabaptists in Munster, Germany or the Puritans in New Haven, Connecticut. Other interpreters, such as John Bunyan and William Blake, adopted a more literary or symbolic understanding of the Apocalypse. The nineteenth century saw the rise of new churches like the Seventh Day Adventists and Jehovah's Witnesses, movements that persist in making end time predictions to this day.

---

[13] See Katherine R. Firth, *The Apocalyptic Tradition in Reformation Britain 1530-1645* (Oxford: Oxford University Press, 1979), 13.

[14] Arthur W. Wainwright, *Mysterious Apocalypse* (Nashville: Abingdon, 1993), 62.

In modern times, most Christian churches profess historic creeds that are clear in their eschatological expectations. The Apostle's Creed anticipates a Jesus who will "come again to judge the living and the dead" and claims belief in "the resurrection of the body"; while the Nicene Creed agrees that Christ "will come again to judge the living and the dead," and proclaims that "we look for the resurrection of the dead, and the life of the world to come."[15] Members of these churches will rarely hear discussion of apocalyptic theology from the pulpit, yet they are constantly inundated by rumors of "the Rapture" and other fantastic interpretations of Revelation from the media. Consequently, many Christians have become suspicious of the book of Revelation and other apocalyptic texts.

---

[15] The Apostles, Nicene, and Athanasian Creeds are the three earliest and most widely used creeds of the Christian Church. The Athanasian Creed agrees with the apocalyptic expectations of the other creeds, but elaborates on them, saying of Jesus that: "He ascended into heaven, he sits at the right hand of the Father, God Almighty, from whence he will come to judge the living and the dead. At whose coming all men will rise again with their bodies and will give an account of their own works. And they that have done good will go into life everlasting; and they that have done evil, into everlasting fire."

True Believers

Yet while some might dismiss the apocalypse as "an idea whose time never comes but is always expected,"[16] many others remain true believers. For example, shortly after September 11, 2001, a Time/CNN poll found that 59 percent of U.S. citizens believe that the prophecies in Revelation will come true, and 25 percent believe that the attacks on the World Trade Center were prophesied in scripture.[17] For regardless of the impact of secular education, science, and modernism, and despite the fact that the end of the world has often been predicted and that the people predicting it have thus far always been wrong, there is actually no way of knowing for certain that an apocalyptic prediction will *not* come true.

Apocalyptic belief today is extraordinarily diverse, appropriating knowledge and symbolism

---

[16] See Deepak Chopra, "The Seduction of Apocalypse," *Huffington Post*, Apr. 7, 2006. "In real-world terms," Chopra continues, "there is no chance that the apocalypse is near, a fact that we will wake up to once reason returns."

[17] See Craig Unger, "American Rapture," *Vanity Fair*, Dec. 2005.

from disparate sources to create diverse and innovative perspectives on the apocalypse. While smart secular scholars like Francis Fukayama speculate on the social convulsions that will precipitate the end of history,[18] blockbusters such as Mel Gibson's *Apocalypto* help maintain the fascination of audiences with apocalyptic predictions of the end of time.[19] Equally compelling are the claims of top scientists and their advocates who forecast that global warming will precipitate an environmental cataclysm that will spell the extinction of the human race.[20] "We have [such] good 'scientific' reasons for expecting the End," claims Richard Landes, Director of Boston University's Center

---

[18] Fukayama's "The End of History and the Last Man" (1992) focuses on the purposelessness of time subsequent to the fall of the Berlin Wall and the anti-communist upheaval in Eastern Europe.

[19] Set in the ancient Mayan empire, Apocalypto (2006) considers the Mayan calculation of "long time," an eerily accurate calendar that predicts that the world will end in 2012, advertising that "When the End Comes, Not Everyone is Ready to Go." Accessed Jan. 10, 2007 <http://apocalypto.movies.go.com/.>

[20] "I am afraid the atmosphere might get hotter and hotter until it will be like Venus with boiling sulfuric acid. I am worried about the greenhouse effect. Unless the human race spreads into space, I doubt it will survive the next thousand years." Stephen Hawking, *Associated Press*, Sept. 30, 2000.

for Millennial Studies, "it is no longer even necessary to believe in God to believe in the apocalypse."[21]

We have such good "scientific" reasons for expecting the End, it is no longer even necessary to believe in God to believe in the apocalypse.

Even so, the religious tradition of Abraham provides a plethora of prophetic and eschatological literature anticipating the apocalypse, of which the book of Revelation is easily the most elaborate narrative depiction.[22] While Hebrew scripture and the Muslim Qur'an can easily be interpreted to denounce the abuses of empire in anticipation of the last days, surely the most comprehensive narrative account of this prophetic tradition is found in the Christian New

---

[21] See Richard Landes, "Apocalypse: A Roundtable Discussion," *Frontline*, Sept. 1999. Accessed Oct. 15, 2006 <http://www.pbs.org/wgbh/pages/frontline/shows/apocalypse/roundtable/tres.html.>

[22] The Synoptic Gospels also hold many apparent predictions of Jesus' return at the end of times, including the Olivet discourse, or Little Apocalypse (Mt. 24, Mk. 13, Lk. 21) and the Parable of the Sheep and the Goats (Mt. 25:31-46, Mk. 8:34-9:1, Lk. 17:20-37).

Testament, particularly in the book of Revelation.[23] Millions continue to follow these traditions to the letter, while many mainline Christians tend to dismiss Revelation as something unintelligible or nonsensical. But to ignore this tradition, or to abandon interpretation of the Apocalypse to nationalistic or self-interested religious fanatics, is to discard one of the church's most powerful means for inculcating discipleship.[24]

Already it may be too late, as, demagogues and despots have been using the rhetorical power of apocalyptic language to great effect in the developing world. A recent example was touted in the news: the day after a United Nations speech by United States President George W.

---

[23] Though this essay emphasizes the Christian tradition, specifically the book of Revelation, it may also hold relevance for Jewish and Muslim apocalypticism. For example, the event represented in Jewish eschatology by the tradition of the blowing of the *shofar* (Lev. 25:9; Ez. 33:6) parallels the "loud voice like a trumpet" that first appears in Revelation 1:10, and is again reflected in the Qur'an when the archangel Israfil blows a blast on his trumpet on the final day of judgment, the Qiyâmah (Qur'an 50:37-42).

[24] See Wes Howard Brook and Anthony Gwyther, *Unveiling Empire: Reading Revelation Then and Now* (New York: Orbis, 1999), 2-4.

Bush, Venezuelan President Hugo Chavez objected to the smell of sulfur in the UN General Assembly hall, and suggested relocating the UN's headquarters to Caracas. "The devil came here yesterday," he observed, to thunderous applause. "Yesterday, ladies and gentlemen, from this rostrum, the president of the United States, the gentleman to whom I refer as the devil, came here, talking as if he owned the world: truly, as the owner of the world. And it smells of sulfur still today, this table that I am now standing in front of."[25]

Authorities were dismayed when Chavez's remarks were met by a "loud applause that lasted so long that the organization's officials had to tell the cheering group to cut it out."[26] Only hours before, Mahmoud Ahmadinejad, President of the Islamic Republic of Iran, had made similar comments lambasting the United States as "the Great Satan," an unremarkable assertion from the

---

[25] "President Hugo Chavez Delivers Remarks at the U.N. General Assembly," *Washington Post*, Sept. 20, 2006.

[26] Helene Cooper, "Iran Who? Venezuela Takes the Lead in a Battle of Anti-U.S. Sound Bites," *New York Times*, Sept. 21, 2006.

leader of this Islamic state.[27] An ardent apocalypticist, President Ahmadinejad has spent millions to refurbish Tehran in preparation for the return of the Mahdi, which will occur, he predicts, by 2008.[28] Yet Chavez, who carries a crucifix wherever he goes, draws his conclusions not from Muslim prophecy, but from his understanding of the bible and the teachings of the Christian faith.[29] "I preach the good news of

---

[27] "Zionists are the true incarnation of Satan," claims Ahmadinejad. "The Zionist regime was created by the British, brought up by the Americans, and commits crimes in the region with their support." "Zionists 'incarnation of Satan,' says Ahmadinejad," *Middle East Times*, Mar. 1, 2007.

[28] Louis Sahagun, "End Times Groups Want Apocalypse Soon," *Los Angeles Times*, Jun. 22, 2006.

[29] Venezuela's oil wealth, insists Chavez: "belongs to all of us. We're going to share it like Christ. ... It will be enough for everyone." See Jorge Rueda, "Chavez deepens Petrocaribe oil pledges," Business Week, Aug. 11, 2007. Chavez backs up this Christian rhetoric with highly visible "humanitarian" action, compelling the Venezuelan state-owned oil company CITGO to provide deep discounts and deferred payments on oil and gas to low-income people throughout the Americas, including 400,000 families in the United States. See Sheldon Alberts, "Chavez uses petro-dollars to help the poor in America," *CanWest News Service*, Dec. 5, 2006.

Jesus Christ," he claims, "[and] a revolt of hope is going on today."[30]

Political and religious leaders the world over continue to interpret Christian and Muslim prophecy to condemn the imperial ambitions evident today in the United States and its leaders.

Chavez's and Ahmadinejad's remarks speak to the increasing ideological alliance between Christianity in the developing world and fundamentalist Islam, at least in their mutual identification and denunciation of the United States as the Great Satan or Babylon of prophecy, and of George W. Bush as *Al-Dajjal* or Antichrist.[31] They and other political and religious leaders the world over continue to interpret Christian and Muslim prophecy to condemn the imperial

----

30 From a lecture at St. Paul & St Andrew UMC church in Manhattan on Sept. 17, 2005. See Finley Schaef, "Venezuela's Pres. Chavez Speaks at SPSAW," Memorial UMC Newsletter, Vol. 10 No. 9, Oct. 2005. Accessed Apr. 6, 2007 <http://www.gbgm-umc.org/memorialny/news100105.html.>

31 "Al-Dajjal," with the definite article, refers to "The Impostor," a specific end-time deceiver.

ambitions evident today in the United States and its leaders.

The specter of this understanding is of increasing concern to the established church/state hegemony in the United States, so much that the politically influential National Association of Evangelicals found it necessary to officially disclaim Chavez' remarks. Determined to set the record straight, NAE President Ted Haggard asserted that, "NAE theologians and scholars have conducted a thorough exegetical study of the biblical texts concerning the person, disposition, and earthy manifestations of Satan .... They have incontrovertibly concluded that, contrary to the assertion of Hugo Chavez, President Bush is not the Devil."[32]

For as any student of prophecy will recognize, the one identified as the "Antichrist" (1 Jn. 2)

---

[32] "President Bush the Devil? Asks National Association of Evangelicals," *Christian Newswire*, Sept. 21, 2006. A frequent advisor to President Bush, Ted Haggard demonstrated his expertise on issues regarding the demonic in late 2006 when he was dismissed over a scandal involving methamphetamine use and prostitution.

must fit a few extremely narrow qualifications.[33] First, he must be a charismatic politician, for it is prophesied that all whose names have not been written in the book of life will worship him (Rev. 13:8); as well as a military commander, for his armies will cover the whole earth, even unto God's holy mountain (Dan. 11:45). What's more, he "uses all power, signs, lying wonders, wicked deception [and] powerful delusion, leading [us] to believe what is false" (2 Thess. 2:10).

President Bush fit these qualifications on many accounts. Yet not long after Ahmadinejad and Chavez made their accusations, the people of the United States elected a new president, one that is routinely referred to in the international press as the "Messiah" and the "President of the World."[34] And like few leaders before him, President Barack Obama, with his million-dollar smile, could be said to exemplify the charisma characteristic of the biblical Antichrist (Rev. 13:8).

---

[33] In the New Testament, the Antichrist is referred to as "the beast" (Rev. 13), "the lawless one" and "the man of sin" (2 Thess. 2). See commentary on Revelation 13.

[34] See "Messianic rhetoric infuses Obama rallies," *Politico*, Dec. 9, 2007, by David Paul Kuhn and Ben Smith.

Describing himself as a "citizen of the world," unlike Bush, Obama's popularity could quite imaginably result in his being followed by "the whole earth" (13:4) and having authority over "every tribe, people, language and nation" (13:7).

Of course, if one were to ask Obama if this was his plan he would claim no knowledge of it, and not because he's unaware of his role and and responsibility. Rather, it is always Satan's plan and Satan's power that animates the Antichrist (13:4). Yet like Nero, Napoleon, Mao, Bush and others, Obama may be only a *type* of antichrist, not the ultimate eschatological Antichrist that Christ will defeat at the battle of Armageddon.

The Bible says that, in the last days, there will be an increase in disasters and apostasy before the Great Tribulation. Then Christ will return with a sword in his mouth to defeat the Antichrist at the battle of Armageddon and establish his millennial kingdom. Revelation's promise of the coming apocalypse certainly provided great hope to early Christians facing torture and persecution in the coliseums of the Roman Empire. In the same way, the apocalypse has functioned as a parable of obedience in suffering for Protestants during the Inquisition, or for Jehovah's Witnesses in the Nazi concentration camps, or for the martyrs "disappeared" in South America, or for Christians massacred by the thousands in Africa's internecine wars, etceteras.

Today, still on this side of the tribulation, the parable of the Apocalypse is as relevant as ever, perhaps more so. Surely this is an unprecedented era, where the juxtaposition of technological advance and moral and cultural decline threaten that the fragile bonds that hold human beings in relationship are in danger of being disintegrated and replaced with a totalitarian New World Order. Socialist George Orwell described this possible future in his classic "1984":

> Already we are breaking down the habits of thought which have survived from before the Revolution. We have cut the links between child and parent, and between man and man, and between man and woman. But in the future there will be no wives and no friends. ... There will be no distinction between beauty and ugliness. ...

> Children will be taken from their mothers at
> birth as one takes eggs from a hen.[35]

In advanced economies like Great Britain and the United States, the state has already taken on the role of father to as many as 40 percent of children. How long until there are no longer any such thing as "fathers," only sperm donors, then how long until mothers are likewise dispensed with, and then how long before this demonic, antiseptic culture is exported all over the world?

The New World Order

This is the promise of a New World Order, in which humans ultimately have no binding relationship to anyone or anything but the faceless state. "If you want a picture of the future," predicts Orwell, "imagine a boot stamping on a human face - forever."[36] Conspiracy theorists suggest that a secret illuminati of socialist elites has been plotting this grim future for humanity, and are even now just

---

[35] George Orwell, *1984* (New York: Signet Books, 1961), 267.

[36] Ibid.

waiting for the right candidate to lead us into their Orwellian nightmare.

If you want a picture of the future, imagine a boot stamping on a human face - forever.

John writes: "Children, it is the last hour! As you have heard, the Antichrist is coming, so now many antichrists have come. From this we know that it is the last hour" (1 Jn. 2.18). Many antichrist figures will arise throughout history - each one recognizable as an inordinately charismatic political and military leader - but only one will be *the* Antichrist of prophecy. Today many prophets and others who interpret scripture are suggesting that President Obama may be actualized as a *type* of antichrist, but whether he is the ultimate Antichrist depends on God's timing and the machinations of the political process, the results of which remain to be seen. In the meantime, "we wait for a new heaven and a new earth, where righteousness is at home" (2 Pet. 3:13).

Hermeneutics: Revelation as Parable

This is a world where there is only one lord and master, where there is only one system. The empire is everywhere. It seems there are no longer any alternatives. - Franz Hinkelammert[37]

Again, the bible does not tell us the specific hour of Christ's return. It does, however, ask Christians to watch and be ready. Mark's narrative reminds us to "Beware, keep alert ... or else he may find you asleep when he comes suddenly" (Mark 13:33-36). Hence, the

---

[37] Franz Hinkelammart, "Changes in the Relationships Between Third World Countries and First World Countries," in *Spirituality of the Third World*, eds. K.C. Abraham and Bernadette Mbuy-Beya (Maryknoll, NY: Orbis, 1994), 10-11.

interpretation of Revelation and other apocalyptic literature is often understood by scholars to be "keeping alert" in anticipation of Christ's return. Conversely, other scholars will study the Apocalypse as a purely academic exercise.

Notoriously complicated and obscurantist, traditional schools of apocalyptic interpretation typically classify their views under innumerable and indecipherable categories, each with its own hermeneutical axe to grind. Whether a biblical interpreter considers herself to be Pre-Tribulational, Hyper-Dispensationalist, Post-Millennial or Partial-Preterist arises out of the historical conditions and concerns of her worshipping community, or lack thereof.

Confusion is avoided by simplifying these categories into a few primary methods of interpretation. Although there is no definitive method of classification, three basic categories encompass most interpretive methods: the "*Academic*" hermeneutic, including historical-critical, aesthetic, and postmodern interpretation; the "*Biblical Prophecy*" hermeneutic, for which Revelation clearly anticipates Jesus' Second Coming; and the *"Actualizing"* hermeneutic, which seeks to find a synthesis between academic method and prophetic interpretation.

The "Academic" Hermeneutic

Academic interpretation of the Apocalypse begins with the historical-critical method, which reads Revelation as a text written for a particular audience in a particular time and place and is thus primarily concerned with questions of historical context.[38] In principle, this perspective eschews most prescriptive interpretations of the Apocalypse in tacit agreement that Revelation is indecipherable outside of its original context.[39] Consequently, many members of the mainline church and the academy prefer to maintain a

---

[38] The historical-critical method attempts to recreate the historical circumstances of the construction of a text and then to ascertain the author's intended meaning from within those constraints.

[39] "Scripture has one meaning," wrote Benjamin Jowett, "the meaning which it had in the minds of the Prophet or Evangelist who first uttered or wrote, to the hearers or readers who first received it." See Benjamin Jowett, "On the Interpretation of Scripture," in Essays and Reviews (7th ed.; London: Green, Longman and Roberts, 1861) 378.

studied silence on Revelation, a silence commonly assumed to imply a rejection of any interpretive hypotheses that propose a correlative reading of the Apocalypse.

As Revelation has so often been read toward nationalistic or xenophobic ends, it is perhaps understandable that academic interpreters hesitate to construe it as anything but an artifact. Utilizing historical-critical method, these scholars read the Apocalypse as a pastoral letter in which, "to the extent that the seer's images can be applied to concrete persons or events or institutions at all, they refer to things and people in the seer's own world ."[40] Of course, this view is corroborated by Jesus himself in what C.S. Lewis called "the most embarrassing verse in the Bible,"[41] in which Jesus claims that "this generation will not pass away until all these things have taken place" (Mt. 24:34).

Broadly summarized, historical-criticism provides a guideline for interpretation through

---

[40] Murphy, 32.

[41] C.S. Lewis, "The World's Last Night," in *The Essential C.S. Lewis* (New York: Simon and Schuster, 1996), 385.

emphasizing the historical context in which the text was written. "A modern interpreter," explains Eugene Boring, "cannot accept any interpretation of the book which its first readers would not have understood."[42] Adela Yarbro Collins concurs, saying that:

> Perhaps the hardest won and most dearly held result of historical-critical scholarship on the Revelation to John is the theory that the work must be interpreted in terms of the historical context in which it was composed. ... Perhaps the most widely held conclusions of this approach are that the beast from the sea of chap. 13 and the woman of chap. 17 represent the Roman Empire in some way. Such allusions to the contemporary ruling power raise the issue of the political perspective expressed in these references.[43]

Consequently, historical-criticism recognizes that for the early church Revelation was a manifesto

---

[42] Boring, 51.

[43] Adela Yarbro Collins, "The Political Perspective of the Revelation to John," *Journal of Biblical Literature* Vol. 96, No. 2, Jun. 1977, 241.

for living as the church in conflict with empire.[44] For, while the historical-critical method does not preclude a reading of the bible that comments on current events, it always demands an interpretation that considers the context of the original audience.

A modern interpreter cannot accept any interpretation of the book which its first readers would not have understood.

Confronted by imperial demands for allegiance, the church as an oppressed community interpreted Revelation as a parable of hope. But after the conversion of Emperor Constantine, empire's guild of theologians began to explain Revelation's parable by pointing their interpretive fingers anywhere but towards their vested interest. "The church no longer saw the demonic as lodged in the empire," explains

---

[44] "The contents of the vision are cryptic and at times bizarre," writes Murphy, "but they clearly involve disapproval of the Roman empire and its political and religious claims." See Murphy, 2.

Walter Wink, "but in the empire's enemies."[45]
Once Christians became servants of the empire, if
they interpreted Revelation at all, it would be not
to subvert the empire but against the "other":
against either the political enemies of the empire
or the "other" living in their midst.

It is precisely these "others" that concern
postmodern criticism; for post-modernism is
primarily concerned with making sure every
voice is heard.[46] For example, the
deconstructionist Jacques Derrida posits "respect
for the other" as his "first rule."[47] Although
postmodernism is itself an umbrella term for
describing myriad disciplines, postmodern
perspectives hold in common an emphasis on
peripheral voices. Postmodern scholarship is a
reminder that no perspective is absolute:

---

[45] Walter Wink, *The Powers That Be: Theology for a New Millennium* (New York: Doubleday, 1998), 90.

[46] This brief investigation of postmodern analysis, as well as the emphasis on historical-criticism, owes much to John Collins, whose "concern for developing an approach to the Bible that takes account of current scholarship as much as possible" influenced this book's methodology. See John J. Collins, *The Bible after Babel: Historical Criticism in a Postmodern Age* (Grand Rapids: Eerdmans, 2005), 134.

[47] Ibid., 152.

interpretation always depends upon the person and the context of the interpreter. For this reason, scholars must be wary of reading the biblical text in such a way that it enshrines one particular interpretation.

Emphasizing Revelation's position as a work of literature, aesthetic and literary modes of interpretation focus on questions of textual structure and form criticism.[48] Identifying the unfamiliar elements in the literary structure of the biblical text allows the modern interpreter insight into the objectives of the author as well as the cultural location of the original audience.

For example, Revelation is heavily influenced by the "combat myth" narrative prevalent in the ancient Mediterranean that depicts a cosmic battle to symbolize the resolution of conflict.[49] By adapting the archaic imagery of the combat myth, the author of Revelation was able to

---

[48] Revelation's literary form, suggests Yarbro Collins, is the key to its interpretation. See Adela Yarbro Collins, *The Apocalypse* (Wilmington, DE: Michael Glazier, 1979), x.

[49] See Murphy, 279-286. The "combat myth," also known as the "myth of redemptive violence," is an ancient cosmology rooted in the Babylonian tale of Marduk and Tiamat.

establish a pattern whereby hearers could reinterpret the events of their world.[50] This numerological pattern is Revelation's primary organizational methodology, typical of the apocalyptic genre. Repetition, as in the recurring cycles of visions, only makes the pattern more apparent. While aesthetic and literary interpretation of the Apocalypse may examine Revelation as a metaphor for contemporary concerns, or consider how eschatological symbolism reveals something about the nature of good and evil, it does not typically promote prophetic speculation.

The "Biblical Prophecy" Hermeneutic

In contrast with these academic approaches is the popular view of Revelation as Biblical Prophecy. Eschewed by many in the mainline church and the academy, this category encompasses innumerable interpretations and is consequently the most widely held apocalyptic perspective, adopted by hundreds of millions of

---

[50] Bernard Batto calls this process "mythopoeic speculation." See Bernard Batto, *Slaying the Dragon: Mythmaking in the Biblical Tradition* (Louisville: Westminster John Knox, 1992), 40.

Christians around the world. For example, all those who affirm the traditional creeds of the church are reading Revelation as prophecy in that they anticipate Christ's return. In order to accommodate the diversity of believers from hundreds of different traditions, the category of Biblical Prophecy must hold together perspectives as seemingly oppositional to each other as the "preterist" view, which holds that most if not all prophecy was fulfilled in biblical times,[51] and the "futurist" view, which reads Revelation as anticipating future events.

The Biblical Prophecy category also encompasses the "historicist" interpretation; a view that reads Revelation's prophecy as describing the history

---

[51] Preterism resembles the historical-critical method in agreeing that the prophecies foretold were intended for that generation, however, historical-critical method generally understands the apocalyptic expectations of the early disciples to be disappointed, while classic preterism sees them as fulfilled in their time. Also known as 'realized eschatology,' preterism is traditionally sub-categorized into 'full' preterism and 'partial' preterism. Full preterism is often branded heretical by Christians who point to the anticipation of Christ's return in the historical creeds of the Church. Partial preterism, on the other hand, suggests that while some of the prophesied events came to pass in the biblical era, their final consummation remains in the future. As it affirms the historic creeds of the church, partial preterism is generally considered to be an orthodox interpretation, though it is vehemently opposed by certain denominational traditions.

of the church and that can be subcategorized into various "dispensationalist" or "millennialist" understandings. Perhaps the best known historicist reading is that of Tim LaHaye's "Left Behind" series, a popular fictionalized depiction of the end times. These books adopt the "pretribulation rapture" position, which cites Revelation 3:10 - "because you have kept my command to persevere, I also will keep you from the hour of trial" - to teach that all Christians, both living and dead, will be secretly "raptured," or snatched up, by Jesus to escape the terrible judgment of the tribulation.[52]

Many evangelicals recognize the day when the United Nations formally recognized Israel, May 15, 1948, to mark the commencement of the final countdown to the end.

After the tribulation, of course, Jesus will again return with all the saints. Some evangelical

---

[52] Originating in Scotland around 1830, and popularized by the *Scofield Reference Bible* of 1909, the pretribulation rapture position teaches that Christ will return in secret before his Second Coming.

critics, concerned that belief in the rapture leaves Christians unprepared for tribulation, point to a lack of scriptural corroboration for this teaching. Moreover, LaHaye and other "purveyors of pop-eschatological literature" freely interpret the book of Revelation as a prophecy of American imperial domination.[53] While popular, this view is particularly perilous, argues Boring, "since it often advocates the necessity of nuclear war as part of God's plan for the eschaton 'predicted' in Revelation."[54]

Pointing to a convergence of "apocalyptic" events in these times, interpreters of biblical prophecy claim that the circumstances are ripe for the Second Coming of Christ. Jesus foretold several signs of the end of the age, including "wars and rumors of wars," "famines and pestilences," and "earthquakes" (Mt. 24:6-7). Biblical prophecy scholars expand upon this prediction by

---

[53] Boring, 49. In his recent book, *American Fascists: the Christian Right and the War on America* (Parsippany, NJ: Free Press, 2007), Chris Hedges draws parallels between what he terms the "dominionist movement" of the Christian Right in the United States and the totalitarian politics of Hitler and Mussolini.

[54] Boring, 49.

incorporating select verses from Daniel, Zephaniah, and Ezekiel to identify the reestablishment of Israel as a sign of the coming apocalypse.[55] Accordingly, many evangelicals recognize the day when the United Nations formally recognized Israel, May 15, 1948, to mark the commencement of the final countdown to the end. For example, Hal Lindsay's bestseller, *The Late, Great, Planet Earth*, famously predicted that the end times would arrive within a generation of Israel's statehood.[56]

In addition, the Biblical Prophecy category includes bizarre interpretations such as those held by the growing number of churches worldwide that see the United States as the incarnation of Babylon. One such interpreter

---

[55] In Luke 21:29-30, Jesus uses the fig tree, a frequent metaphor for Israel, to announce the Second Coming, saying: "Look at the fig tree and all the trees; as soon as they sprout leaves you can see for yourselves and know that summer is already near."

[56] See Hal Lindsey, *The Late Great Planet Earth* (Grand Rapids: Zondervan, 1998), 42-59. Lindsey did much to propagate the perspective, popular among Christian nationalists, that plans to rebuild the Jerusalem temple on the current site of the Dome of the Rock as a requirement for Christ's return. A new book by Lindsay, *The Everlasting Hatred: The Roots of Jihad*, revises his prediction to suggest that the Apocalypse will begin with a Muslim attack on Israel triggered by events at the Temple Mount.

reserves harsh criticism for clergy who fail to interpret Revelation as a prophecy for today, writing that: "It is not God who forgot America in prophecy. It is not God who failed to paint a picture that is not obvious to those that wanted to find it. It is not God, but the false prophets of America who have utterly failed their flock."[57]

Those who interpret Revelation as prophecy often insist that these are the last days, the end times, and that therefore reading the Apocalypse is no longer an "academic" exercise. For this reason, prophetic interpreters occasionally condemn the more "academic" interpreters for abdicating the faith, comparing them to the scoffers in 2 Peter 3:3-6, which predicts "that in the last days scoffers will come, scoffing and indulging their own lusts and saying, 'Where is the promise of his coming?'"

Academic methods of biblical scholarship, however, are not intended to immobilize the text, but instead to allow the bible to speak more clearly. Exegetical strategies including historical-

[57] Robert Howard, "Is America Babylon?" *Wake up, America* [online posting]. Accessed Dec. 7, 2005 <http://www.theforbiddenknowledge.com/hardtruth/america_babylon.>

criticism, postmodern scholarship, and aesthetic and literary interpretation can be helpful in crafting an operative hermeneutic that enables the reader "to understand contemporary realities by holding them up alongside images from the Apocalypse."[58] For example, popular readings of Revelation that willfully neglect historical-critical interpretation are often stymied by a failure to acknowledge the most elementary principles of academic scholarship, such as the fundamental literary theory of "recapitulation," which suggests that: "parts of Revelation review things that happen in other parts and restate them or look at them from different perspectives"[59]

Suspicious or ignorant of such biblical scholarship, literalist and fundamentalist interpreters often advocate outrageously incoherent schemes for making sense of the Apocalypse. "Common sense tells us," claims one radio evangelist, "that once something is

---

[58] Kovacs and Rowland, 248.

[59] Murphy, 257. The prominence of recapitulation in the Apocalypse is most evident in the "trumpets" and the "bowls," two cycles of visions that so closely parallel one another that they must describe the same events.

destroyed it is gone. For the two Babylons to be the same, the system would have to be destroyed twice, and that makes no sense whatsoever."[60] However, academic biblical scholarship recognizes that "common sense," or the modern interpreter's cultural perspective, is in this case irrelevant to the interpretation of the text. Instead, historical-critical method and literary criticism allow modern readers to identify Revelation as organized, not chronologically, but in keeping with an ancient literary genre.

The "trumpets" and the "bowls" are two cycles of visions that so closely parallel one another that they must describe the same events.

Reading recapitulation into Revelation at last allows the interpreter to read the book as a consistent whole, though it may frustrate efforts to "decode" the Apocalypse into a clear map of future events. However, attempting to "decode" Revelation by setting specific dates for when

---

60 David Bay, "Economic Babylon of Revelation 18 May Be America," The Cutting Edge [radio program] aired on Aug. 22, 1992. Accessed Dec. 7, 2005 <http://www.cuttingedge.org/ce1038.html.>

apocalyptic events will happen limits the text to one particular interpretation. The obvious danger of "decoding" interpretations is demonstrated in the example of William Miller, whose followers liquidated their assets in anticipation of Jesus' return on a day in 1843 that Miller calculated from the book of Daniel.[61] "When that date arrived and passed," records Justo Gonzalez, "most of Miller's followers left him."[62]

The "Actualizing" Hermeneutic

To the "actualizing" interpreter, however, any exact prediction of the last days is of limited interest. Recognizing that "about that day or hour no one knows" (Mk. 13:32), actualizing the Apocalypse does not trouble with "decoding" specific predictions of an end time date (setting

---

[61] Miller's movement survived under the direction of Ellen G. White, whose prophetic teaching remains relevant for more than 15 million Seventh Day Adventists in the world today. Interpreting Revelation's parable of Babylon, White wrote: "One nation, and only one, meets the specifications of this prophecy; it points unmistakably to the United States of America." See Ellen G. White, *The Great Controversy Between Christ and Satan* (Altamont, TN: Harvest, 1888), 465.

[62] Justo Gonzales, *The Story of Christianity: The Reformation to the Present Day* (Peabody, MA: Prince Press, 1999), 256.

precise dates for when apocalyptic events will happen). Instead, the actualizing hermeneutic is primarily concerned with fleshing out the biblical text in relation to the contemporary context in order to unveil the truth behind the façade. In this way, the lens of the Apocalypse can allow the interpreter to understand present-day circumstances to be an actualization of the events depicted in the book of Revelation.

One nation, and only one, meets the specifications of this prophecy; it points unmistakably to the United States of America.

In that it seeks to find meaning for modern hearers in the biblical text, actualizing interpretation bears some resemblance to the school of biblical prophecy; however, the actualizing interpreter's careful attention to scholarship should mitigate any temptation to decode the Apocalypse. Concern for the principles of the historical-critical method, for example, assures that the actualizing interpreter does not ignore the context in which the text was written. As a result, any actualization of a biblical text must be one that its original audience would have understood. In the case of the Apocalypse to John, a letter directed to early churches suffering Roman persecution, the original context is one of affliction under the rule of empire. An actualization of the text must reflect this context, meaning that Revelation's intended audience is the same today as it was when it was first written: churches suffering under or anticipating tribulation from imperial oppression.

Actualizing thus reads Revelation as a parable. Honoring the book's original meaning in the biblical context, this hermeneutic thus allows the Apocalypse to inform understanding of contemporary events and to provide guidance for life today.[63] Adopting a "double vision" that is both general and specific; the actualizing interpretation does not allow an image or text from the Apocalypse to be identified solely with

---

[63]See Kovacs and Rowland, 9.

one particular situation or person.[64]   The
opposite of decoding, actualizing allows for a
non-objective interpretation that does not limit
the text to one particular circumstance, but
allows the text to be actualized again and again,
so long as it is faithful to its original context.[65]

A notable use of the actualizing hermeneutic is
found in John Calvin's attempt to make sense of
Matthew 24:34, that "embarrassing" text that
appears to insinuate that Jesus himself
anticipated an immanent Second Coming. In his
endeavor to bring this notorious text into line
with the rest of the New Testament, Calvin
discerned a method by which the bible may be
actualized in many times and places, writing that:
"while our Lord heaps upon a single generation
every kind of calamity, he does not by any means
exempt future ages from the same kind of
sufferings, but only enjoins the disciples to be

---

[64] This concept of a "double vision" can be credited to Jacques
Ellul, whose 1977 commentary *Apocalypse* provides a lucid model of
the actualizing hermeneutic. See Jacques Ellul, *Apocalypse: The Book
of Revelation* (New York: The Seabury Press, 1977), 189.

[65] See Kovacs and Rowland, 149-151.

prepared for enduring them all with firmness."[66]
Calvin's coherent use of this actualizing
hermeneutic firmly established a means of
biblical interpretation by which the bible can
speak across generations and continents to
encourage Christians in diverse circumstances.

A more contemporary actualizing interpreter,
Jacques Ellul bridged traditional categories of
interpretation to claim that Revelation holds a
"double vision." Consider John's vision of the
beast rising from the sea in Revelation 13:1. In
their original context, certain aspects of this
vision were understood to allude directly to
Rome; i.e. the beast's seven heads were
interpreted as seven Caesars.[67] But Rome did not
fall, at least not in the way that was expected,
and thus the Apocalypse became the subject of
countless interpretations attempting to transcend
its historical specificity. Ellul suggests that:

---

[66] John Calvin, *Commentary on a Harmony of the Evangelists,
Matthew, Mark, and Luke, vol.3*, tr. William Pringle, (Grand Rapids:
Eerdmans, 1949), 151-152.

[67] Murphy, 296-306.

Rome is not first of all Rome ... Rome is an actualized symbol ... the beast itself is the power ... [and] the woman is seated upon the beast (then she rests in her historical actuality upon the political power! She is a historic actualization of the Power). There is, then, a *double vision*: this political power which has a constant reality and the exercise of power in different forms and with diverse durations throughout the course of history.[68]

Some historical-critical scholars are skeptical of such an "unhistorical" interpretation; for while academics may appreciate an actualizing interpretation for allowing Revelation to speak to people in all times and places, Ellul has often been criticized for "minimizing the specific historical references in Revelation to its first century readers."[69] However, an actualizing interpretation, with its emphasis on maintaining this "double vision," is a reading that allows

---

[68] Ellul, 189.

[69] Boring, 48.

Revelation to hold in tension historic and symbolic aspects of the text.

To say that Revelation is a parable does not imply that it is not true; rather, it recognizes it can be true in many contexts, particularly the current one.

Although the actualizing hermeneutic does not invite any decoding of the text, it does invite the interpreter to examine the parallels between her own era and the era in which John wrote the Apocalypse. For example, because Revelation was understood in its original context to be a condemnation of empire, when actualizing the text it is essential to consider just how Revelation's criticism pertains to the greatest empire the world has ever seen. In this way, Revelation can be understood as a parable for America today, just as it was a parable for Germany under National Socialism or for the Roman Empire in ancient times. To say that Revelation is a parable does not imply that it is not true; rather, it recognizes it can be true in many contexts, particularly the current one.

The actualizing hermeneutic is intended to find a mediating position between exacting academic scholarship and wild-eyed biblical prophecy. Consequently, an actualizing interpretation is not threatened by the use of exegetical tools, but rather embraces them, recognizing the wisdom that contemporary biblical scholarship lends to understanding the text. Using postmodern scholarship - by recognizing that everyone has a power-seeking agenda, for example - demonstrates why interpretations of Revelation serving to protect the interests of class, privilege and empire usually identify the enemy with those in opposition to empire's status quo; and, conversely, why interpretations that arise from communities living in opposition to the state authority and consequent power structure usually identify the enemy as the state or empire ordering their persecution.[70]

Again, it is possible to discern the most historically accurate interpretation with the help of the historical-critical method, which suggests that the authentic, "original" reading of

[70] See Collins, 12.

Revelation is inevitably one in conflict with empire, as opposed to one compromised by empire. Utilizing these exegetical methods, the actualizing interpreter is better able to understand the political perspective from which the book was written, and consequently is equipped to faithfully read the Apocalypse in relation to contemporary circumstances.

Taken together, the "*Academic*" disciplines (historical-criticism, postmodern scholarship, aesthetic interpretation) can moderate the "*Biblical Prophecy*" tradition to inform an "*Actualizing*" method of reading Revelation, offering guidelines to establish a framework for dialogue. Using the actualizing hermeneutic to frame the discussion of a biblical text does not discourage reading the text to remark upon new circumstances, but allows for a reading to remain true to the author's perceived intent, simultaneously attending to a plurality of interpretive perspectives.

To read Revelation as a parable allows a faithful interpretation in conversation with the modern context, while avoiding the temptation to interpret according to motivations of personal agenda or civil religion.[71] Furthermore, framing the interpretive discipline in the context of a "dialogue" or "discussion" or "conversation" demonstrates that biblical scholarship does not intend to prove ontological truth claims; instead, establishing this hermeneutic is intended to create the parameters of a dialogue in which all participants can agree upon the context, if not the content, of the interpretation.

---

[71] See Ibid.

Actualizing Babylon

Fallen, fallen is Babylon the great! ... for your merchants were the magnates of the earth, and all nations were deceived by your sorcery. And in you was found the blood of prophets and of saints, and of all who have been slaughtered on earth.
- Revelation 18:1, 23-24

H ow odd it seems to us," observes William Stringfellow, "that the death of a society - especially, perhaps, the violent disintegration of this most rich and powerful of all nations: Babylon - should incite jubilation in heaven."[72] Yet this is the hope proclaimed in the book of Revelation: "Hallelujah! The smoke goes up from [Babylon] forever and ever!" (Rev. 19:3). How can it be that Revelation so rejoices in Babylon's demise?

Babylon as Metaphor

To the biblical imagination, Babylon - the location of the fabled Tower of Babel -was the very embodiment of wickedness.[73] In 586 B.C.E. Nebuchadnezzar destroyed the Jerusalem temple and forced the Israelites into captivity in Babylon, a time that spawned the witness of prophets such as Jeremiah and Ezekiel.[74] Renowned among the ancients for its splendor (the Ziggurat, the Hanging Gardens, the Ishtar Gate), Babylon was made immortal in the Old

---

[72] William Stringfellow, *An Ethic for Christians and Other Aliens in a Strange Land* (Eugene, OR: Wipf and Stock Publishers, 2004), 25.

[73] The first mention of Babylon in the Old Testament is found in Genesis 11; however, it is only in the books of Kings and Isaiah that historically significant material can be found. See Duane Watson, "Babylon," in *Anchor Bible Dictionary* I, 563.

[74] Exile raised theological questions for the Israelites about how to worship God in a distant land, after the temple was destroyed. Jeremiah, Ezekiel and others arose in order to speak to these concerns.

Testament as the quintessential sphere of idolatry under the control of Satan. Meanwhile, Babylon's celebrated King Nebuchadnezzar, famous throughout the ancient world as a "superfigure who was either a god or godlike,"[75] was remembered by the prophets of Israel for being murderous and cruel: Nebuchadnezzar was rumored to have made a favorite drinking cup out of the skull of a murdered Jew. After Babylon's fall, the Jews became vassals of Persia, who encouraged them to return to Palestine and rebuild the temple and the city of Jerusalem as a bulwark against Egypt.

Nebuchadnezzar was rumored to have made a favorite drinking cup out of the skull of a murdered Jew.

Fast forward five hundred years to 70 CE, when the temple in Jerusalem is destroyed again, utterly and for the last time, by the Roman

---

[75] See Ronald H. Sack, "Nebuchadnezzar," in *Anchor Bible Dictionary* IV, 1059.

legions.[76] This event, plus the many inherent similarities between Rome and ancient Babylon, led naturally to their comparison: for like Babylon, Rome was the wealthy capital of a great empire; like Babylon, Rome cruelly persecuted God's covenant people; like Babylon, Rome required its subjects to worship idol gods; and like Babylon, Rome claimed celestial authority for its exploits.[77] Early Christians, however, as followers of the crucified one, had eyes of faith to see that Rome had acquired its empire not by divine mandate, but by the ruthless violence of

---

[76] Flavius Josephus records that, "While the Temple was ablaze, the attackers plundered it, and countless people who were caught by them were slaughtered. There was no pity for age and no regard was accorded rank; children and old men, laymen and priests, alike were butchered; every class was pursued and crushed in the grip of war, whether they cried out for mercy or offered resistance." See E. Mary Smallwood, *Josephus: The Jewish War*, translator G.A. Williamson (London: Penguin, 1981), 367.

[77] Babylon demanded the worship of idols: in Daniel 3, Shadrach, Meshach, and Abednego refuse to worship Nebuchadnezzar's idol and are condemned to be burned alive. Likewise, Rome commanded its subjects to worship a plethora of gods, including the emperor, who was considered divine. For example, an inscription of Caesar Augustus proclaims: "The most divine Caesar . . . who being sent to us and our descendants as Savior, has . . . become [god] manifest." See Richard A. Horsley, *Jesus and Empire: The Kingdom of God and the New World Disorder* (Minneapolis: Augsburg Fortress, 2002), 23-24.

its military strategy.[78] The enemy of the church, Rome was clearly in the service of Satan; therefore, Rome was seen to be the very actualization of Babylon.

Satan and the Demonic

Frequent reference to Satan, though largely unintelligible to a contemporary audience, constituted powerful rhetoric in the era in which the Apocalypse was written. Satan is thus alluded to by numerous designations throughout the book of Revelation: as "Satan" (2:9; 2:13; 2:24; 3:9; 12:9; 20:2; 20:7); "the devil" (2:10; 12:12; 20:2); "the dragon" (12:3; 12:7; 12:13; 12:15-18; 13:1; 13:4; 13:11; 16:13; 20:2); "the serpent" (12:9; 12:15; 20:2); "Abaddon" or "Apollyon" (9:11); and "the accuser" (12:10).[79] Moreover, Satan does not act

---

[78] At the burning of Sepphoris, for example, around the time of Jesus' birth, the Roman military crucified 2,000 Jewish rebels simultaneously. See Richard A. Horsley and Neil Asher Silberman, *The Message and the Kingdom: How Jesus and Paul Ignited a Revolution and Changed the Ancient World* (Minneapolis: Augsburg Fortress, 2002), 11.

[79] John names two apostate churches "synagogue[s] of Satan" (2:9; 3:9), while claiming that another church studies "the deep things of Satan" (2:24). Numerous other references in Revelation refer to Satan's abode, called "Hades" (1:18; 6:8; 20:14) and "the bottomless pit" (9:1; 20:1).

alone, but rather enlists the service of "demonic spirits" (16:14), the most terrible of which is called "the beast" (11:7; 13:2; 13:11; 17:7; 19:19).

Though these terms might seem archaic, even meaningless to someone with a modern worldview, they reflect the experience of first century Christians who encountered what they considered a demonic power in the machinations of the Roman Empire.[80] "Humans naturally tend to personalize anything that seems to act intentionally," explains Walter Wink. "Anyone who has lost computer files to a virus knows how personal this feels. [Something similar was] what it was that people in ancient times were experiencing when they spoke of "Satan," "demons," "powers," "angels," and the like."[81]

Stringfellow provides a more exacting definition, suggesting that "demonic refers to death

---

[80] "In the ancient worldview, where earthly and heavenly reality were inextricably united," writes Walter Wink, "this view of the Powers worked effectively. But for many modern Westerners it is impossible to maintain that worldview." Wink, *The Powers That Be*, 26.

[81] Ibid., 27. "I prefer to think of the powers as impersonal entities," claims Wink, "though I know of no sure way to settle the question." Ibid.

comprehended as a moral reality, [while] to be possessed of a demon means to be captive to the power of death."[82] While death assumes many different manifestations, in the Gospel story the demonic forces are not only the authors of illness, madness, and temptation; demons are also the controlling power behind Herod, Caiaphas, Pilate, and other religious and imperial overlords.

> *We might think of "demons" as the actual spirituality of systems and structures that have betrayed their divine vocations.*

The Bible claims demons can have no influence over humans beings unless they are able to embody themselves in people (see Mk. 1:21-25; Mt. 12:43-45; Lk. 11:24-26), pigs (Mk. 5:1-20), or political systems (Rev. 12-13).[83] "We might think of

---

[82] Stringfellow, *An Ethic for Christians*, 32. "Physical or mental illnesses are frequent and familiar examples," elaborates Stringfellow, "but the moral impairment of a person (as where the conscience has been retarded or intimidated) is an instance of demonic possession, too."

[83] See Wink, *The Powers That Be*, 27.

'demons' as the actual spirituality of systems and structures that have betrayed their divine vocations," suggests Wink.[84]   In the same way, Satan can be identified as the all-pervasive ethos of domination that rules over the individual powers.

The Principalities and Powers

Christ's conflict with these demonic forces is typically summarized in the non-narrative Epistles as a conquest over the "principalities and powers," as, for example, in Colossians 2:15: "He disarmed the principalities and powers and made a public example of them, triumphing over them in him."[85] The Bible teaches that the principalities and powers are part of God's created order, intended for good: "for in him all things in heaven and on earth were created, things visible and invisible, whether thrones or dominions or rulers or powers" (Col. 1:16). Karl Barth interprets this text to mean that the governments of nation-states, as the preeminent

---

[84] Ibid.

[85] See James McClendan, *Systematic Theology: Ethics I* (Nashville: Abingdon Press, 1986), 174.

principalities, "should serve the Person and the Work of Jesus Christ, and therefore the justification of the sinner" by upholding the "commonly acknowledged law giving equal protection for all."[86]

It is only natural for the nation-state to bear some resemblance to the kingdom of God, as the state exists as an earthly counterpart to the heavenly City. "The state," claims Barth "is an allegory, a correspondence and an analogue to the kingdom of God which the church preaches and believes in."[87] The state thus claims a spiritual power over persons, explaining why "people who have been deeply influenced by these traditions have an

---

[86] See Karl Barth, *Church and State* (London: SCM, 1939), 29. See also Romans 13:1-2: "Let everyone be subject to the governing authorities, for there is no authority except that which God has established. The authorities that exist have been established by God. Consequently, whoever rebels against the authority is rebelling against what God has instituted, and those who do so will bring judgment on themselves."

[87] Quoted in Haddon Wilmer, "Karl Barth," *The Blackwell Companion to Political Theology*, eds. Peter Scott and William T. Cavanaugh (Malden, MA: Blackwell, 2004), 131.

almost sacred view of constitutional government and of human rights."[88]

However, these powers – all earthly powers – are fallen, or alienated from God, because they choose to serve themselves rather than God's larger purpose. By way of example, the authority of the modern nation-state is acknowledged as an irrefutable fact of existence, to which the work of the church must be adapted. This blind allegiance is confirmed in times of war, when the church routinely acquiesces to the state by allowing Christians to kill and torture other human beings, often other Christians, for whatever cause the state determines.[89] As Stringfellow explains, "A nation or other principality may be such a dehumanizing influence ... may be of such an antihuman

---

[88] See Max Stackhouse, "Public Theology and Democratic Society," in *The Church's Public Role: Retrospect and Prospect*, ed. Dieter T. Hessel (Grand Rapids: Eerdmans, 1993), 65.

[89] See William T. Cavanaugh, *Torture and Eucharist: Theology, Politics, and the Body of Christ* (Malden, MA: Blackwell, 1998), 7-9. "What this looks like in practice," recognizes Cavanaugh "is the case of the bishop ... who can speak a word to the conscience of the Catholic soldier, but cannot override the soldier's orders from his army superior to torture his fellow Christians." Ibid., 9.

purpose and policy ... that it must be said that the nation ... is governed by the power of death."[90]

Babylon represents the essential version of the demonic in triumph in the nation.

Such is the implication of the parable of Babylon in Revelation: "Babylon represents the essential version of the demonic in triumph in the nation," interprets Stringfellow.[91] Describing a dragon that calls forth a beast from the sea and a beast from the land, Revelation 13 delineates between the empire (as represented by the beasts) and Satan (represented by the dragon that conjures the beasts). The beast from the sea and the beast from the land allude to the Roman policy of ruling through puppets, such as Herod, backed

---

[90] Stringfellow, *An Ethic for Christians*, 32.

[91] Ibid., 32.

up by the empire's pervasive military presence.[92] "Behind the empire stands Satan," elucidates Frederick Murphy, and "the empire itself is best represented by a supernatural beast of chaos."[93] Walter Rauschenbusch made a similar interpretation, writing that: "the Empire is described as the creature and agent of the Satanic power."[94]

Intriguingly, secular philosopher Michel Foucault is also in agreement with these claims of Revelation. "The political, ethical, social, philosophical problem of our days," claims

---

[92] "The first beast is worshipped along with the dragon (13:4), and the job of the second beast is to enforce that worship ... the responsibility of the ruling class in Asia Minor." See Murphy, 309. Today, the US has a similar reputation for cultivating puppet regimes in "developing" nations: consider Batista in Cuba, Somoza in Nicaragua, Trujillo in the Dominican Republic, the Duvaliers in Haiti, Marcos in the Philippines, Diem in Vietnam, Suharto in Indonesia, and now Karzai in Afghanistan and whoever is in Iraq.

[93] Murphy, 332.

[94] Yet, in his era, Rauschenbusch could observe "no such world wide power of oppression as the Roman empire." See Walter Rauschenbusch, *A Theology for the Social Gospel* (Nashville: Abingdon Press, 1990), 88-89. This may have been true in 1917, yet today "the US has accumulated more power than Charlemagne, the Roman Empire, and Britain at its imperial height." See Ziauddin Sardar and Merryl Wyn Davies, *Why Do People Hate America?* (New York: Disinformation Co., 2002), 111.

Foucault "is not to try to liberate the individual from the state and from the state's institutions, but to liberate us both from the state and from the type of individuation which is linked to the state."[95] Foucault concurs with Revelation: not only must persons be liberated from the empire and its institutions but also from the spiritual powers behind them, distinguishable from the institutions themselves like the dragon is from the beast.

Although ancient, these powers were only beginning to be recognized in a time in which Roman institutions and bureaucracies were tightening their grip over people's daily lives. Two thousand years later, these same powers are still operating in the service of empire, like "faceless functionaries staffing a huge and heedless machine."[96] Writes Wink: "It was this sense of being caught up in the maw of some colossal force beyond human control that first led

[95] Michel Foucault, "The Subject and Power," in *Michel Foucault: Beyond Structuralism and Hermeneutics*, by Hubert Dreyfus and Paul Rabinow (Chicago: University of Chicago Press, 1982), 216.

[96] Wink, *The Powers That Be*, 38.

to the discovery of the principalities and powers."[97]

Like Foucault, Revelation wants to make clear that the conflict is between both physical and metaphysical realities. Things are not what they seem. But while these powers and principalities are much stronger than individual humans, Revelation proclaims that Christ has broken the back of the demonic authorities. The powers are not invincible as they claim; rather they are doomed, and it is only a matter of time before they are destroyed.

> *The powers are not invincible as they claim; rather they are doomed, and it is only a matter of time before they are destroyed.*

The author of Revelation illustrates these powers by using fantastic descriptions of creatures he calls "dragon," "leopard," and "beast." Remarkably, modern people still follow this practice by using animal symbols to refer to

[97] Ibid., 39.

institutions: i.e. the bulldog represents Yale, the eagle the United States, and "the pig the police."[98] "If some of these [images] seem quaint," Stringfellow makes it clear that "transposed into contemporary language they lose all quaintness and the principalities become recognizable and all too familiar. They include all institutions, all ideologies ... all idols. Thus the Pentagon or the Ford Motor Company or Harvard University ... are all principalities."[99]

The typical human response to these powers is to submit to their authority. "In most cultures," writes Bruce Bradshaw, "the oppressed want to overcome their oppression by being grafted into the structures."[100] Confronted with the apparently unshakable authority of these institutions, people generally assume that the only way to survive is to conform. "Overwhelmed by the incomprehensible size of corporations,

----

[98] Stringfellow, *An Ethic for Christians,* 78.

[99] Ibid.

[100] Bruce Bradshaw, *Bridging the Gap: Evangelism, Development, and Shalom* (Monrovia, CA: World Vision International, 1993), 148.

bureaucracies, universities, the military, and media icons," explains Wink, "individuals sense that their only escape from utter insignificance lies in identifying with these giants and idolizing them as the true bearers of their own humanity."[101]

Yet by joining with the oppressive powers, individuals may "lose a part of their humanity; [as] the structures define who they are and the decisions they make."[102] Barth voiced this concern on behalf of German Christians in the 1930's, suggesting "that they took Hitler as dominant fact, to which Jesus the Savior was to be adopted as a flexible, subordinate metaphor."[103] The German Christians of that era exalted Hitler for bringing recovery to Germany and insisted that all the Protestant churches combine forces in a national renewal under his guidance. "It was this scenario," recalls Haddon Wilmer, "that prompted Barth's notorious 'Nein'; for the condition of the church in German society

---

[101] Wink, *The Powers That Be*, 60.

[102] Bradshaw, 148.

[103] See Willmer, 132.

was such that a distinction needed to be drawn, saying 'No' to false connections of church and political movement, of faith in God and national belonging."[104]

---

[104] Ibid., 128.

Exegesis: Redefining Reality

The real political task in a society such as ours is to criticize the working of institutions which appear to be both neutral and independent; to criticize them in such a manner that the political violence which exercises itself obscurely through them will be unmasked, so that one can fight them.
- Michel Foucault[105]

T he Book of Revelation was written to redefine the nature of reality for its audience. Proclaiming a true account of reality, in contrast to the propaganda taught by

---

[105] Michel Foucault, "Human Nature: Justice versus Power," in *Reflexive Water: The Basic Concerns of Mankind*, ed. Fons Elders (London: Souvenir Press, 1974), 171.

worldly authorities, Revelation offers a reinterpretation of events that challenges the dominant propaganda, proposing a narrative of existence that offers a radical alternative to the status quo. Threatened by persecution at the hands of the Empire, early Christians were tempted to "worship the beast" by capitulating to the demands of the state.

To name is to define and control. By renaming things, Revelation changes the world for its audience.

John's Apocalypse challenged their perspective, equipping people to reinterpret the events of their time so as to see that the supposed glory and power of empire is but a monstrous approximation of divine power and authority. The power of Revelation is in this sense the power to name, regardless of the context in which it is heard. "To name is to define and control," writes Murphy. "On an earthly level, Rome has authority to name. Our author, by renaming things, changes the world for his audience."[106]

More poetry than prose, if Revelation is interpreted "literally" rather than figuratively, prognosticating about current events may result in misunderstanding. Yet for those who are subject to what is potentially the most powerful empire the world will ever know, Revelation is the New Testament book that is most germane to our current political situation.[107] Written for those living under the domination of empire, Revelation declares Christians to be subject to a single authority by making a prophetic counterproposal to the state's claims to loyalty, thereby revealing any pretension to authority on

---

[106] Murphy, 356

[107] Claiming that Christian faith is essentially apolitical, many Christians cite Paul's only clear statement on political responsibility in Romans 13:1: "Be subject to the governing authorities; for there is no authority except from God"). Yet, as Ogletree argues, "this constraint [to be subject] can be ignored … where we judge the society's normative framework to be functionally idolatrous." See Thomas Ogletree, *The World Calling: the Church's Witness in Politics and Society* (Louisville: WJK Press, 2004), 40.

the part of earthly powers to be false.[108] Efforts to interpret the Apocalypse disclose that Revelation is not about conveying information per se; instead, Revelation functions as a parable: challenging its audience's preconceptions so as to change the way they see the world.[109]

Revelation is framed by two beatitudes: the first, blessing those who "hear and who keep ... the words of the prophecy" (1:3); and the last, blessing "the one who keeps the words of the prophecy of this book."[110] The demand that the hearers "keep" or "hold" the prophecy indicates a concern that the audience will fail in this task. Clearly, "what is to be held is not simply information or doctrine," claims Murphy, but "a

---

[108] "The state's claim to loyalty is expressed above all in the claim upon citizens that they may and indeed must kill in wartime." See Stanley Hauerwas, *Dispatches from the Front* (Durham, NC: Duke University Press, 1994), 106.

[109] See Frederick J. Murphy, *Fallen is Babylon: The Revelation to John* (Harrisburg, PA: Trinity Press International, 1998), 56.

[110] "Beatitudes like 'Blessed are you poor, for yours is the kingdom of God' (Luke 6:20) imply that the kingdom does not belong to the rich," writes Murphy. "Revelation fits into this prophetic tradition. For John, the powerful are about to fall; the oppressed vindicated. The world is not as it appears." Murphy, 63.

moral stance, a way of life that must be guarded against the encroachments of the evil world."[111]

 As a result, Revelation seems to be less concerned with passing on factual knowledge than in altering the way those who hear it perceive the world. The power of an actualizing hermeneutic is that it allows the Apocalypse to be understood as holding a message for one place in time without being strictly bound to that particular situation. By reflecting on Revelation's original context, as well as recognizing that any application of the text constitutes but one possible actualization of the narrative, an actualizing hermeneutic can make it possible to plausibly interpret the Apocalypse in light of contemporary concerns.

The Apocalypse follows an established framework, closely adhering to the timeline of events established in the synoptic gospels (Mt. 24; Mk. 13; Lk. 21). This simple storyline eventually became the literary template for the book of Revelation, for the narrative is reduplicated almost exactly. Forecasting first

---

[111] Ibid.

deception ("Many will come in my name and say, "I am he"" (Mk. 13:6)); then "wars," "earthquakes," and "famines" (Mk. 13:7-8); then betrayal ("children will rise against parents and have them put to death" (Mk. 13:13)); then suffering ("suffering such as has not been since the beginning of the creation" (Mk. 13:19)); then cataclysm ("the sun will be darkened" (Mk. 13:24)); the apocalyptic narrative culminates in "the Son of Man coming in clouds with great power and glory [to] gather his elect" (Mk. 13:26). Revelation begins with this blueprint of a storyline and develops it into a complete narrative account replete with fantastic visions and numeric patterns of reduplication, skillfully structured in an effort to retool the audience's perception of the cosmic order.

Behind it all is the clearly identifiable backdrop of the ancient combat myth, deliberately adapted by Revelation's author to provide hope for a people in desperate circumstances.[112] Yarbro Collins describes the combat myth as adhering to

---

[112] The "conscious extension of older mythic symbols to new political realities," writes Bernard Batto, "was what we [today] would call philosophizing or theologizing." Batto, 40.

a typical pattern, in which "one of the combatants is usually a monster, very often a dragon. This monster represents chaos and sterility, while his opponent is associated with order and fertility."[113] With the monster's destruction, order is restored. Order thus dominates over chaos by means of violence: might makes right, war makes peace, and religion exists in order to perpetuate the status quo. Accordingly, whoever dominates over another earns the favor of the gods. "The myth of redemptive violence is the simplest, laziest, most exciting, uncomplicated, irrational, and primitive depiction of evil the world has ever known," claims Walter Wink.[114] The hallmark of any "dominator society," this myth is as commonly accepted and believed in the modern era as at any time in history.

By combining aspects of several versions of the ancient myth, the author of Revelation created a revised combat myth that turned the ancient

[113] Adela Yarbro Collins, *The Combat Myth in the Book of Revelation* (Missoula, MT: Scholar's Press, 1976), 57.

[114] Wink, *The Powers That Be*, 53.

cosmology on its head. Scandalously, in Revelation's adaptation of the combat myth, the ones who "conquer" are not the dominators, but their victims! "Those who conquer" (Rev. 21:7) are "those who have been beheaded for their testimony to Jesus and for the word of God. They had not worshipped the beast or its image and had not received its mark on their foreheads or their hands. They came to life and reigned with Christ a thousand years" (Rev. 20:4).

> *Scandalously, in Revelation's adaptation of the combat myth, the ones who "conquer" are not the dominators, but their victims!*

Using signs, symbols, and literary methods familiar to him, Revelation's author spoke to his situation while simultaneously preserving the possibility for his book to be interpreted to the present day. Towards this purpose, Revelation is organized, not chronologically, but numerologically, constructed largely around the mystical number seven.[115] Seven golden lampstands represent seven churches and seven angels become seven stars in the hand of the Son of Man. There are seven seals on the heavenly scroll, seven trumpets of tribulation, and seven bowls full of seven plagues. There are many less explicit series of sevens, such as the seven beatitudes, and a literary structure consisting of a recurring pattern of seven unnumbered visions; so many sevens, in fact, that scholars speculate that the Apocalypse was influenced by "a well-developed Pythagorean speculative tradition on the number seven."[116] The second most prevalent number in Revelation, twelve, is significant to Christians because of the twelve apostles and the

---

[115] There are seven days of creation, for example, and seven days of the week, of which the seventh is sacred. As numbers are seen to elude meaning more symbolic than a mere calendar date, numerological structure is yet another aspect of the Apocalypse that discourages "decoding" predictions.

[116] Adela Yarbro Collins, *Cosmology and Eschatology in Jewish and Christian Apocalypticism* (Leiden: Brill, 1996), 97. Pythagoras believed that everything was related to mathematics and that, through mathematics, everything could be predicted and measured in rhythmic patterns or cycles.

twelve tribes of Israel.[117] These numbers, argues Yarbro Collins, are intended to "make visible the will of God and Christ which stands behind and directs all events. They are, as it were, the net in which the Satanic forces are captured, surrounded, and confined."[118]

Often used in Jewish and Christian writings of that era, numerology is a structural device typical of the apocalyptic genre.[119] The aforementioned principle of reduplication is another numerological aspect of this genre. Although Revelation was written as a work of prophecy, its literary form is considered to be apocalyptic in part because numbers provide the key to

---

[117] Twenty-four elders sit on twenty-four thrones in heaven, while 144,000 will be redeemed from humankind. The New Jerusalem measures 144,000 cubits and has twelve walls seated on twelve foundations inscribed with the names of the twelve apostles. The twelve walls of the city contain twelve pearly gates that are inscribed with the names of the twelve tribes and guarded by twelve angels.

[118] See Yarbro Collins, *Cosmology and Eschatology*, 137.

[119] "Apocalypses," writes Yarbro Collins, are "intended to interpret present, earthly circumstances in light of the supernatural world and of the future, and to influence both the understanding and behavior of the audience by means of divine authority." Yarbro Collins, ed., "Early Christian Apocalypticism: Genre and Social Setting" *Semia 36: An Experimental Journal for Biblical Criticism* (Atlanta: Scholar's Press, 1986), 7.

unlocking its organizational scheme.[120] Unique in that the numerology is so explicit, one could say John's apocalypse belongs to a category all by itself.[121] Nevertheless, Revelation still falls under the literary category of apocalypse in that it attempts to "remove the cover" in order to encourage the audience to understand current events from a divine perspective.

Introductory Verses (1:1-1:9)

"The Revelation of Jesus Christ" could be considered the actual title of this book, for this was John's title in verse 1 of the original manuscript. The title explains its origins, and in the style of the ancient prophetic books, John's title then elaborates that it is a direct revelation from God, who "sent his angel to his servant, John" (1:1). The emphasis here is that this message is the very word of God, "made

---

[120] Elisabeth Schussler Fiorenza suggests that Revelation "must be valued as a genuine expression of early Christian prophecy whose basic experience and self-understanding is apocalyptic." Elisabeth Schussler Fiorenza, *The Book of Revelation: Justice and Judgment* (Philadelphia: Fortress, 1985), 140.

[121] Yarbro Collins, *Cosmology and Eschatology*, 19-20.

known" (1.1) to John who testified "even to all that he saw" (1.2).

The first of seven beatitudes is introduced here in verse 3 - "blessed is the one who reads aloud the words of this prophecy" - which reminds us that the book was designed for use in Christian worship. This initial series of seven beatitudes (1:3; 14:13; 16:15; 19:9; 20:6; 22:7; 22:14) this is the first indication that the structure of this book is built around series of sevens. Verse 3 concludes with the assurance that "the time is near," a consistent theme of Revelation (see also 2:16; 2:25; 3:11; 3:20; 6:11; 10:6; 11:2-3; 12:6; 12:12; 17:10; 22:6; 22:7; 22:10; 22:20). Today, two thousand years later, Christians still continue to wait on God's promises, recognizing "that with the Lord one day is like a thousand years, and a thousand years are like one day" (2 Pet. 3:8).

John addresses his letter in verse 4 to the "seven churches that are in Asia," before continuing with a greeting in standard Pauline form - "grace to you and peace" - though John makes a point of recognizing here that God is the one who still "is to come" and that "seven spirits ... are before his throne." Verse 5 introduces Jesus Christ as "the faithful witness, the firstborn of the dead, and the ruler of the kings of the earth," all titles that will be important to the unfolding narrative. The familiar liturgical passage in verse 7 ("Look! He is coming with the clouds ...") is an allusion to Daniel 7:13 applied to Jesus as the coming Son of Man (see also 14:4; Mk. 8:38; 13:26). The clear message is that Christ is coming soon and that this is reason for "all the tribes of the earth to wail" (1:7). This introductory section concludes with the very voice of God pronouncing: "I am the Alpha and the Omega" (1:8), or the first and last letters of the Greek alphabet, inferring that God has authority over the end as well as the beginning.

Seven Messages for Seven Churches (1:9-3:22)[122]

After these introductory verses (1:1-1:9), John then describes himself and the circumstances of his revelation. A fellow believer suffering persecution on the island of Patmos, John "was

---

[122] This organizational methodology is adapted from Murphy, who borrows Yarbro Collins' divisions.

in the Spirit on the Lord's day" (1:10) when he heard "a loud voice like a trumpet" telling him to "Write in a book what you see and send it to the seven churches" (1:11). Revelation then relates a vision of "one like the Son of Man" (1:13) surrounded by seven golden lampstands (1:12) and holding seven stars in his hand (1:16), again emphasizing the importance of the number seven to Revelation's organizational scheme. He had hair as white as wool (1:14), with a two-edged sword coming out of his mouth (1:16), and his face was shining like the sun (1:16).

This terrifying figure of the cosmic Christ then asks again for John to write a message to seven churches. While some believe that those named were actual churches of the era; other scholars suggest that all churches of all times can be comprehended in these seven, representing completeness, particularly as Christ is surrounded by seven angels on behalf of the seven churches.[123]

---

[123] Another prevalent interpretation is that of "dispensationalism," first propagated in the nineteenth century by John Nelson Darby, which interprets these seven churches as referring to seven successive stages of church history according to covenant promises explicated in the Old Testament.

In fact, the messages in Rev. 1:19-3:22 are issued, not to the churches themselves, but to these same "angels of the seven churches" (1:20), an early indication that Revelation is concerned primarily with unseen powers and spiritual realities: "For our struggle is not against enemies of blood and flesh, but against the rulers, against the authorities, against the cosmic powers of this present darkness, against the spiritual forces of evil in the heavenly places" (Eph. 6:12).

Scholars suggest that all churches of all times can be comprehended in these seven, representing completeness.

Again, from an actualized hermeneutic, these messages can be considered as directed not only to those historic churches but to the angels of seven different types of churches, relevant across all of history and even to this day. Examining each of these messages in turn, the actualizing reader can expect to glean some wisdom for the contemporary church.

A. *The Message to Ephesus (2:1-7)*

Probably the most important city in the Roman province of Asia, Ephesus was a port and an intersection for the Roman Empire and a center of the imperial cult. Addressed to the angel of the church and recorded as the very words of Jesus, the body of the letter begins, as do all seven letters, with the words "I know": in this case, "I know your works, your toil, and your patient endurance" (2:2). This is something very significant, for these words declare that the cosmic Christ is intimately aware of the concerns of these small churches in Asia Minor, a thought that surely was affirming to the struggling community.

The Ephesian church is praised also for its refusal to tolerate evildoers, its testing of false apostles, and its patient endurance (2:2-3). Even so, Christ criticizes them because they have "abandoned the love [they] had at first" (2:4). Although they do much that is right, their lack of love still condemns them. The cosmic Christ then threatens that if they do not repent, then he will "remove [their] lampstand from its place" (2:5), which seems to suggest that Ephesus will no longer be a church. This will happen even though Christ again praises this church because they "hate the works of the Nicolaitans, which I also hate" (2:6).[124] Orthodoxy is important, yes, but orthodoxy without love counts for nothing.

Anecdotally, the situation of the church in Ephesus seems very like many churches today that claim rigorous doctrinal standards and clearly condemn any error in interpretation, but who are perhaps cold toward strangers and others who do not fit the image of what the church feels is appropriate, making assessments that may have much more to do with cultural standards than with gospel standards. Sadly, this describes many devout church communities today that are heavy on piety but light on hospitality. Although Christ praises Ephesus more than he does many of the other churches, his harsh message to the church indicates that if

---

[124] Irenaeus believed that the Nicolaitans were followers of Nicolaus of Antioch, a proselyte who was among the seven men chosen to serve the Jerusalem congregation (Acts 6:5), who had forsaken true Christian doctrine; he said they lived in unrestrained indulgence (*Against Heresies 1*; 26:3). However, to my knowledge there is no contemporary historical reference point to the Nicolaitans outside of these two passages in Revelation (2:6, 2:15).

they don't repent, they remain in grave danger of being separated from him.

B. *The Message to Smyrna (2:8-11)*

One of only two messages that are entirely positive (the other is to Philadelphia), the message to Smyrna appears to be written to prepare the church for persecution and a season in which some of them may die. Christ says to the church in Smyrna, "I know your affliction and your poverty, even though you are rich" (2:9). It appears that, although the church suffers material poverty, they are spiritually rich, as evidenced by the approval of Christ's message to them.[125] Later in Christ's message, the church at Laodicea receives the opposite judgment, for while it seems to be rich and prosperous, it is truly poor (3:17).

The city of Smyrna was known for its respected population of Jews, and later Christian tradition recalls the Jews of Smyrna as hostile to the

---

[125] It is possible that the church was poor because of their faithfulness to Christ, as was the church referenced in Hebrews that "cheerfully accepted the plundering of your possessions, knowing that you yourselves possessed something better and more lasting" (Heb. 10:34).

Christians there.[126] The tension between the church and the Jews is spelled out as "slander on the part of those who say they are Jews and are not, but are a synagogue of Satan" (2:9). This designation "synagogue of Satan" is unique to Revelation, occurring nowhere else in Jewish or Christian literature.[127] The promised "ten days" of affliction (2:10) recalls the ten days during which Daniel and his companions were allowed to live as Jews in the Babylonian court (Dan. 1:12-13). "Be faithful unto death," Christ promises, "and I will give you the crown of life" (2:10). James, too, refers to the "crown of life" promised to one who resists temptation (Js. 1:12), yet this promise recalls the one made to the Ephesian church that they might eat of the "tree of life" in the paradise of God (2:7).

---

[126] The *Martyrdom of Polycarp* and the *Acts of Pionius* claim that Smyrna's Jews had a hand in the deaths of Polycarp (d. ca. 155 C.E.) and Pionius (d. ca. 250 C.E.).

[127] Murphy, 123.

C. The Message to Pergamum (2:12-17)

The message to Pergamum is similar to the message to the church in Ephesus in several ways. In both, Christ both praises and condemns the church, and both have dealings with the heretical Nicolaitans. Yet while Ephesus is praised for condemning the group, Pergamum is criticized for tolerating it. In this case, if the church does not repent of its error, Christ threatens to come and "make war against [some of] them with the sword of my mouth" (2:16). Here, Christ declares his intention to use the sword of his mouth to divide heretical Christians from faithful ones, recalling the parable of the wheat and the chaff (Mt. 3:12).

While John's vivid description of a vast network of evil forces may not be scientific, it does resonate with our experience.

Pergamum is referred to as "where Satan's throne is" and "where Satan lives" (2:13). A mainstream feature of New Testament teaching, the personification of evil as Satan - "the accuser" (12:10) - might seem something of an anachronism in the twenty-first century. Yet while John's vivid description of a vast network of evil forces may not be scientific, it does resonate with our experience. When it comes to evil, "cosmic" is not too big a word, and "dragon" not too bizarre an image.[128] For as the author of the letter to the Ephesians makes clear: "We do not wrestle against flesh and blood" (Eph. 6:12). Those who conquer - the martyrs, those faithful unto death - will receive "some of the hidden manna and a white stone [on which] is written a new name ..." (2:17), the meaning of which is obscure.

D. The Message to Thyatira (2:18-29)

Strangely, the longest message was addressed to what was the least important of the seven cities.[129] The only prior New Testament reference to Thyatira was the mention of a convert named Lydia, who was "from the city of Thyatira and a dealer in purple cloth" (Acts 16:14). In some ways

---

[128] See Boring, 167.

[129] Charles (by way of Murphy, 123).

the church in Thyatira was the opposite of the church in Ephesus: for where Ephesus is condemned for losing the spirit of love, Thyatira is praised for having love even greater than before; and where Ephesus rejects the false apostles, Thyatira accepts them. Yet the cosmic Christ has one primary concern about Thyatira: that they "tolerate that woman Jezebel, who calls herself a prophet" (2:20). It has been argued that this passage is evidence that the seer of Revelation was unable to accept female leadership in the church (see 1 Tim. 2:11-15). But if John is against female leadership *per se*, he never says so. Instead, he opposes Jezebel's teaching.

Surely the name Jezebel was not one this person chose, but one that was chosen for her as an allusion to the biblical Jezebel, of whom Jehu said, "What peace can there be, so long as the many whoredoms and sorceries of your mother Jezebel continue?" (2 Kings 9:22). Jezebel's heretical teaching seemed to advocate eating food offered to idols and teaching her followers to practice fornication, which may be a reference to many kinds of impurity. Interestingly, Christ says that he "gave her time to repent, but she refuses to repent of her fornication" (2:21), yet another indication of God's being patient with us.

Jezebel's teachings are called the "deep things of Satan" (2:24), which compels me to make reference to a modern day church leader that may represent an actualized corollary to Jezebel of Thyatira. The Rev. Dr. Katherine Ragsdale, President and Dean of the Episcopal Divinity School in Cambridge, MA, uses her bully pulpit to promote the obscene message that abortion is a "blessing"; that those who provide it are saints, that providing abortions is holy work, and that we need more of it, not less. What follows is an excerpt from her sermon entitled, "Our Work Is Not Done":

> "When a woman becomes pregnant [and] decides she does not wish to bear a child; and has access to a safe, affordable abortion - there is not a tragedy in sight -- *only blessing*. These are the two things I want you, please, to remember - abortion is a blessing and our work is not done. Let me hear you say it: abortion is a blessing and

our work is not done. Abortion is a blessing and our work is not done. Abortion is a blessing and our work is not done."[130]

Here I reduplicate a large portion of Ragsdale's teaching in order to illustrate the audacity of her position, which certainly speaks for itself. That the Episcopal Divinity School would appoint to its highest administrative post the author of such a grotesque teaching seems evidence of a sordid influence over the entire institution. Now a generation of Episcopal priests is being taught that abortion is a "blessing." Is Katherine Ragsdale a contemporary actualization of Jezebel teaching the "deep things of Satan"?

E. *The Message to Sardis (3:1-6)*

The church in Sardis apparently had a "name of being alive" (3:1), but in fact was dead; meaning that it had a good reputation, but that the

---

[130] Ragsdale continues, "I want to thank all of you who protect this blessing ... who put your lives on the line to care for others (you are heroes - in my eyes, you are saints); the escorts and the activists; the lobbyists and the clinic defenders; all of you. You're engaged in holy work". Quoted by Randy Sly, "From New President of Episcopal Divinity School: Abortion is a Blessing", Catholic Online, April 3, 2009 at <http://www.catholic.org/national/national_story.php?id=32962.> This more contemporary reference, updated since 2007, is the only actualization I did not include in my original graduate thesis.

reputation was undeserved. Christ acknowledges that most Christians think that the Sardian church is spiritually "alive," but that he sees things differently. There is no specific explanation of why the church in Sardis is dead, only that Christ has determined it to be so. Thus Sardis's situation is the opposite of Smyrna's: Smyrna may soon die, but is promised that it will live; while Sardis is thought by many to be alive, but in fact it is already dead.

For Revelation, "to conquer" equals martyrdom.

Still, a few people in the Sardian church remain faithful, described as having "not soiled their clothes; they will walk with me, dressed in white, for they are worthy" (3:4). Here is a more extended description of the rewards to those who conquer: "you will be clothed like them in white robes, and I will not blot your name out of the book of life" (3:5). The white robes are the same as those worn by the martyrs under God's altar in verse 6:11, and lends weight to the interpretation that, for Revelation, "to conquer" equals martyrdom. The book of life refers to the Old

Testament tradition of God's book, for God has made it known that "whoever has sinned against me I will blot out of my book" (Ex. 32:32). Already, the stage is being set for the final judgment as prophesied by Daniel, in which the Ancient One and his heavenly court sit in judgment, "and the books were opened" (Dan.7:10).

F. *The Message to Philadelphia (3:7-13)*

Christ's message to the church in Philadelphia is, again, one of only two messages without condemnation (the other being to Smyrna). Philadelphia and Smyrna were also similar in that they both suffered grave disagreements with the Jews. Here also the primary concern comes from "those of the synagogue of Satan who say they are Jews and are not" (3:9). Proving his authority in this case, Jesus emphasizes his possession of "the key of David" (3:7), perhaps the same keys that Jesus describes as "the keys to the kingdom of heaven" (Matt. 16:19). Yet not only does the cosmic Christ have the keys to the door, he *is* the door by which everyone must enter (John 10:7-9).

"Look, I have set before an open door, which no one is able to shut" (3:8).

Because the Philadelphian church has proved itself faithful, Christ promises to "keep [them] from the hour of trial that is coming on the whole world to test the inhabitants of the earth" (3:10). Christ's promise is that he will make of them "a pillar in the temple of my God" and will write on them "the name of my God, and the name of ... the new Jerusalem ... and my own new name" (3:12). It is not completely clear what Christ's "new name" means, though it may be the same as the secret name inscribed on the white stone given to the conquerors in the message to the church in Pergamum (2:17).

G. *The Message to Laodicea (3:14-22)*

The church in Laodicea is mentioned several times in Paul's letter to the Colossians, establishing that Paul worked for both churches (2:1). Colossians also mentions that Paul had written a letter to the church in Laodicea (4:16), though no such letter survives today. The message to Laodicea is similar to that to the church in Sardis that in both cases it is difficult to determine exactly what was happening, yet these two messages are the most negative of the seven. In both churches, things are apparently going well. Again, the church in Laodicea receives the opposite judgment of the church in Smyrna; for while the Laodocean church says, "I am rich, I have prospered, I need nothing," Christ condemns them as "wretched, pitable, poor, blind, and naked" (3:16).

Christ's criticism that the Laodiceans are "lukewarm" is a fitting indictment of many of our churches today.

Christ's criticism that the Laodiceans are "lukewarm" (3:16) is a fitting indictment of many of our churches today. A contemporary actualization could recognize similar churches in every city and town in the United States: churches that have become so content with their established routine to the point where they more resemble a country club than the body of Christ. The term "C and E" Christians was coined to describe those who attend just twice a year, though for many contemporary Christians in America even that would be a stretch. Today, many self-described Christians on church membership lists are so lukewarm in their participation in the worship and life of the church that it could be argued that they are not Christians at all, as they show no evidence of a connection to the larger body of Christ.

Christ concludes his message to the churches with a warning: "Listen! I am standing at the door, knocking; if you hear my voice and open the door, I will come in" (3:20). His words again reiterate that it is not too late to answer his knock and open to door to salvation and eternal life. As already evidenced numerous times in these messages, God's mercy is great and God gives his people numerous chances to repent and to return to him. Even the cataclysm that is coming is but further evidence of God's concern for us, for as Christ explains: "I reprove and discipline those whom I love" (3:19).

Each of these messages concludes with a promise made to the "one who conquers," or to those that die in the faith.[131] Those who conquer will "eat from the tree of life that is in the paradise of God" (2:7); they will "not be harmed by the second death" (2:11); they will receive "hidden manna" and a "new name" (2:17); they are given "authority over the nations" (2:26) and granted "the morning star" (2:28); they will be dressed in "white robes" and will have their name preserved in the "book of life" (3:5); they will be made "a pillar in the temple of God" (3:12); and reserved "a place on [Christ's] throne" (3:21).

> *Not all Christians will suffer martyrdom, but all must face the prospect of it.*

There is some disagreement on whether only martyrs will inherit the promised eschatological rewards, or whether these promises are made to

---

[131] Again, to "conquer" in Revelation means exactly the opposite of what it means to conquer in human terms; for example, "They have conquered him [Satan] by the blood of the Lamb and by the word of their testimony, for they did not cling to life even in the face of death" (Rev. 12:11).

all who are faithful to the end.[132] Regardless, the message here is that Christians must be prepared to resist the powers of evil unto death, even if they are not martyred. "Not all Christians will suffer martyrdom," explains Caird, "but all must face the prospect of it."[133]

The Heavenly Throne Room (4:1-5:14)

Next, John's perspective broadens as he travels to heaven "in the spirit" (4:2) to witness to a fantastic eschatological cycle of visions. A door opens in heaven to reveal a heavenly throne room, an image that recalls Ezekiel's vision by a river in Babylon,[134] as well as the aforementioned throne room scene from Daniel 7 in which the one seated on the throne looks like the cosmic

---

[132] For example, while Charles claims that only martyrs will conquer, Caird interprets Revelation to say that these promises are to be given to all faithful Christians. See R.H. Charles, *A Critical and Exegetical Commentary on the Revelation of St. John, v.1* (Edinburgh: T. and T. Clark, 1920), 54; also George B. Caird, *The Revelation of St. John the* Divine (London: Andam and Charles Black, 1966), 33.

[133] Ibid.

[134] As Revelation describes, "around the throne is a rainbow that looks like an emerald" (Rev. 4:3), while the throne Ezekiel saw had a "splendor like a bow in the clouds on a rainy day" (Ez. 1:28).

Christ in Rev. 1:14: "his clothing was white as snow, and the hair of his head like pure wool; his throne was fiery flames, and its wheels were burning fire" (Dan. 7:9). Here in Revelation chapter 4, however, the one seated on the throne "looks like jasper and cornelian" (4:3) but is otherwise barely described. This one is attended by twenty-four elders may represent the union of the twelve tribes of Israel and the twelve apostles. That these elders wear crowns and white garments, sit on thrones, and exercise authority suggests that they represent faithful martyrs who have already "conquered."[135]

The four living creatures attending the throne are among the most fantastic depictions in a book full of strange characters: the first like a lion, the second like an ox, the third with a human face, and the fourth like an eagle (4:6-9). Their description borrows heavily from Ezekiel, as well as from Isaiah and Daniel. Ezekiel describes "four living creatures" as being "of human form, with each having four faces: the face of a human being, the face of a lion on the right side, the face

---

[135] See Murphy, 180.

of an ox on the left side, and the face of an eagle" (Ezek. 1:10). The vision in Revelation describes four creatures each with different faces, but the idea is the same. Also, as in Isaiah's vision, each of the four living creatures has six wings - not four - and together they praise God unceasingly, singing "Holy, holy, holy" (Isa. 6:3).

The one seated on the throne then produces a scroll sealed with seven seals (5:1). To John's audience this scroll would be evocative of Daniel's prophecy of the end times; a vision that the angel Gabriel had commanded Daniel to seal years before, saying, "But you, Daniel, keep the words secret and the book sealed until the time of the end" (Dan. 12:4).[136] It appears no one can open the scroll, until John notices a figure standing in the throne room "as if it had been slaughtered" (5:6), a figure with seven eyes and seven horns that is simultaneously "Lion" (5:5) and "Lamb" (5:6). As the figure takes the scroll from the hand of God, the elders and creatures fall down and worship him, singing, "You are

---

[136] See also Ezekiel 2:8-3:3.

worthy to take the scroll ... worthy is the Lamb that was slaughtered" (5:9, 12).

The Seven Seals (6:1-8:5)

The Lamb opens each seal in turn, and as each seal is broken something happens. The breaking of the seals inaugurates the beginning of tribulation on the earth, while the order of these events corresponds with Jesus' apocalyptic predictions in the synoptic gospels.[137] Opening the first four seals conjures up four riders on horseback, often referred to as the Four Horsemen of the Apocalypse, surely the most lampooned characters from Revelation throughout history.[138] A recent Google search ("four horsemen apocalypse") displayed as the most popular image result a cartoon portraying

---

[137] Compare with Rev. 6:2-17, 7:1; also Mk. 13:7-9, 24-25; Lk. 21:9-12, 25-26. See Charles, 158. Such close similarities in events and in order make a case that the author of Revelation depends on an established tradition predicting the endtime, either the synoptic gospels themselves or a common source.

[138] There are similarities to Zechariah 1:10, in which he describes a vision of a rider with four horses – two red, one sorrel, and one white – called "those whom the LORD has sent to patrol the earth." Later, Zechariah sees four chariots: the first pulled by red horses, the second by black horses, the third white horses, and the fourth dappled grey horses. See Zech 6:2-3.

"The Four Horsemen of the (Current) Apocalypse": George W. Bush ("Ignorance"), John Ashcroft ("Intolerance"), Donald Rumsfeld ("War") and Dick Cheney ("Greed").[139]

The author of Revelation depends on an established tradition predicting the endtime, either the synoptic gospels themselves or a common source.

Riding as a conqueror on a white horse, some see the first horseman as an image of Christ; while others view this figure as antichrist. Widespread anticipation of a coming deceiver - see Mt. 24:5 and 2 Thess. 2:8-11 - would seem to indicate that the first horseman is the expected Antichrist. Although he resembles the Christ of chapter 19, this horseman holds a military bearing and weapon, while Christ's victory is in his suffering and death. The name "Antichrist" is not used in Revelation; however, the first horseman, the beast of the sea, and other images in Revelation of an evil counterpart to Christ appearing at the

---

[139] Anonymous cartoon [online posting]. Accessed Mar. 18, 2007 <http://z.about.com/d/politicalhumor/1/0/S/Y/ bush_horsemen.jpg.>

end of time correspond to the character of the "man of sin" from 2 Thessalonians and the "king of the north" of the ancient prophecies of Daniel. The character of the Antichrist will be more thoroughly examined and actualized in the commentary on the two beasts of Revelation 13.

The second horseman, wielding a "great sword" (6:4), rides a red horse, symbolic of the slaughter of the war he brings to the earth. A black horse carries the third rider, who holds a set of scales, accompanied by a voice from heaven saying, "A quart of wheat for a day's pay, and three quarts of barley for a day's pay, but do not damage the olive oil and the wine!" (Rev. 6:6). These are exorbitant prices, eight to sixteen times the normal price for grain, yet oil and wine are unaffected. These circumstances would favor the rich, while placing an unfair burden on those who live hand to mouth; indeed, it would be hard for the poor even to eat at these prices.[140] Such little grain for a day's wages represents an unjust pay scale far below subsistence level, a situation analogous to that of the modern era in which most of the world's workers earn only pennies

---

[140] See Charles, 166-167.

per day; meanwhile oil and wine, the two commodities most important to those who enjoy a high standard of living, continue to flow unabated. The fourth horseman, riding a "pale green horse" (6:7), is Death, "and Hades followed with him" (6:8), to bring famine and pestilence and destruction over one-quarter of the earth.

Actualizing this text into our modern context recognizes that, in many respects this scenario is descriptive of the state of the world today. According to UN development reports, in the year 2000: "2.4 billion people did not have access to adequate sanitation; 1.2 billion people were living on less than $1 equivalent per day; 1.0 billion people lacked access to improved water resources; and 10.7 million children age five or younger died of preventable diseases such as malaria, tuberculosis, and cholera."[141]

The focus of the fifth seal returns to the heavenly throne room to expose the souls of the martyrs under the altar of heaven, crying out for vengeance. This passage intends to make clear

----

[141] See Mary Jane Freeman, "UNDP Report: A Needless Decade of Despair: Developing Nations Are Dying," *Executive Intelligence Review*, Aug. 1, 2003.

that the martyrs are in heaven and will be vindicated by God in and through the eschatological events that follow.[142] They are told to "rest a little longer, until the number will be complete both of their fellow-servants and of their brothers and sisters who were soon to be killed as they themselves had been killed" (6:11). This text indicates that God has preordained a certain number of martyrs and that the world will not come to an end until that number is reached.[143] Such an understanding of martyrdom places a grave obligation on individual believers to resist evil unto death.

To actualize this text into the modern context requires great courage, for here is potentially the point at which the events of Revelation will be set into motion. In fact, this text more than any other may help us to determine the time of

---

[142] See Murphy, 211. A parallel can be found in 1 Enoch 47, in which it is said that "There will be days when all the holy ones who dwell in the heavens will dwell [together]. And with one voice, they shall supplicate and pray on behalf of the blood of the righteous ones which has been shed. Their prayers shall not stop from exhaustion … until judgment is executed for them."

[143] Paul uses a similar argument in Romans 11:25, claiming that "the full number of the Gentiles" must hear the gospel before Israel converts.

Christ's return, for it gives us the formula by which God will decide when to initiate the final consummation. According to this passage, God tells the martyrs whose souls cry out from under his altar to wait "until the number would be complete both of their fellow servants and of their brothers and sisters who were soon to be killed as they themselves are killed" (6:11). This suggests that God has predetermined the number of martyrs and is waiting for this number to be made complete.[144]

God has preordained a certain number of martyrs and the world will not come to an end until that number is reached.

For those who believe that abortion takes a human life, and that at least some percentage of those unborn babies may well be recognized by

---

[144] "We must defer to others' lives," writes James Burtchaell, "not just to avoid the penalties of law, nor merely because every human being has a right to his or her life, right which deserves priority over every other human right, need or desire. We must defer for still another reason: if we deal unjust injury or violent death to others, we shall bring upon ourselves a death of the spirit - a violent death. Those who kill, die. And they die when they slay, not later." James Burtchaell, *Rachel Weeping and other essays on abortion* (Toronto: Life Cycle Books, 1982), 321.

God to be martyrs, recent developments in politics and technology seem now to be conspiring to crank out martyrs as if on a global assembly line.[145] Already doctors in the U.S. perform over one million abortions every year, as they have for the past thirty-five years. The final nail in the coffin could be the proposed national health care legislation that will enshrine abortion as a "right" guaranteed to all American women at taxpayer expense.[146] Again, God is only waiting until the legions of martyrs at rest under heaven's altar reach a predetermined number before the events of the Apocalypse will be inaugurated.

---

[145] "It is terribly important that we give the basic protection of life-loyalty to *all* fellow humans," continues Burtchaell, "not only to those who suit us as valuable contributors to society. No one should have the right or power to decide what qualities or what usefulness others must have to avoid being killed. It is enough to *be* any human being, no matter how burdensome or troublesome, to merit the right to life." Ibid., 322.

[146] Recommendations for increasing access to abortion services under the proposed new national health care plan include: "Eliminate waiting period requirements; Make training in abortion a routine part of medical training; Guarantee confidential access to abortion services for minors; Restore Medicaid funding for abortion; Ensure that private insurance plans cover abortion services." See "Recommendations for Policies and Programs," *Abortion in Women's Lives*," eds. Boonstra et al. (New York: Guttmacher Institute, 2006), 32.

The stage is now set for the opening of the sixth seal, precipitating a deluge of catastrophic eschatological events in which the very "sky vanished like a scroll rolling itself, and every mountain and island was removed from its place" (6:14). The events described here share a long tradition in Jewish apocalypses and biblical prophecy. For example, Isaiah 34:4 predicted that "the host of heaven will rot away, and the skies roll up like a scroll." The people run in fear to hide in what remains of the mountains and rocks, "for the great day of [God's] wrath has come, and who is able to stand?" (6:17).

An interlude occurs between the sixth and seventh seal in which 144,000 servants of God are marked with a seal to protect them from the coming tribulation (7:1-8). It would seem that, while the events of the first five seals affected Christians and non-Christians alike, later plagues do not affect those who bear the protective name of God.[147] The number 144,000, or twelve squared times one thousand, is numerologically symbolic, and is thought to represent the number

---

[147] See Elisabeth Schussler Fiorenza, *Revelation: Vision of a Just World* (Minneapolis: Fortress, 1991), 62.

of martyrs who will experience the first resurrection.[148] An elder tells John that "these are they who have come out of the great ordeal; they have washed their robes and made them white in the blood of the Lamb" (Rev. 7:14).

Later, John sees these same 144,000 standing with the Lamb and it is explained to him that these are those who are already "redeemed from humankind as first fruits for God and the Lamb" (14:5). Left behind to suffer the coming tribulation, the Christians remaining on earth are represented by innumerable multitudes in white robes rejoicing in praise to God before the heavenly throne (7:9-17).

The Seven Trumpets (8:6-11:19)

Opening the seventh seal causes a brief silence in heaven, heightening the anticipation and inaugurating another series of visions in which seven angels blow seven trumpets. The sound of the trumpet indicates the presence of God, and a trumpet blast is associated with the coming of the eschaton throughout the New Testament. For

---

[148] See Boring, 130.

instance, Matthew says of Jesus' second coming, "He will send out his angels with a loud trumpet call" (Mt. 24:37), and Paul writes, "For the Lord himself ... with the sound of God's trumpet, will descend from heaven, and the dead in Christ will rise first" (1 Thess. 4:16).

Chernobyl can be translated into English as "wormwood," which suggests to many that the bible foretells a coming nuclear holocaust.

Each of the first four trumpet blasts is accompanied by a plague: the first brings a plague of hail and fire; the second turns the sea to blood; the third poisons the waters with wormwood[149]; while the fourth destroys a third of the sun, moon and stars. The trumpet that causes the waters to be poisoned with wormwood deserves special attention, for here is a potential actualization with the modern context. After the nuclear accident at Chernobyl in the former

---

[149] "The Ukrainian word for wormwood, a bitter wild herb used as a tonic in rural Russia [is] chernobyl". See "The Talk of Moscow; Chernobyl Fallout: Apocalyptic Tale and Fear," by Serge Schmemann, *Special to the New York Times*, July 26, 1986.

Soviet Union in 1986, the plague of the third trumpet became, for some, a prediction of nuclear disaster. Chernobyl can be loosely translated into English as "wormwood," which suggests to many that the bible foretells a coming nuclear holocaust. Yet nuclear disaster in not the only means by which humanity could be poisoned by radiation. Recent concern over cell phone use causing brain tumors has suggested a new way by which humanity could be poisoned by nuclear radiation on a mass scale.[150]

With the fifth trumpet, a star (angel) falls from heaven to unlock the abyss, which brings a plague of stinging "locusts" with human faces and tails like scorpions. In Revelation, the abyss, or "bottomless pit," is conceived as a temporary place of punishment for fallen angels and demons. Later, in Rev. 20:1, an angel returns from heaven to lock Satan away in the abyss for

---

[150] Studies show a 70% increased risk of grade III–IV astrocytomas (highly aggressive brain tumors) for analog cell phone users. This same study found a nearly 4-fold increase in risk for acoustic neuromas after 15 years of exposure to analog cell phones. See "Tumour risk associated with use of cellular telephones," Lennart Hardell et al., *World Journal of Surgical Oncology*, Oct. 11, 2006. Accessed online <https://www.ncbi.nlm.nih.gov/pmc/articles/PMC1621063/>.

Christ's thousand year reign.[151] The plague of "locusts" recalls Ex. 10:4-20, except that these locusts are demonic and otherworldly, having as their king "the angel of the bottomless pit" (9:7-11). Then the blowing of the sixth trumpet activates four more angels that command a huge army of supernatural cavalry troops on fire-breathing horses. Together these plagues destroy a third of humankind; however, those remaining still "did not repent of the works of their hands, or give up worshipping demons and idols" (9:20).

There is another interlude between the sixth and seventh trumpets in which an angel gives a little scroll to John and tells him to eat it (10:9-10). The scroll tastes sweet but makes John's stomach bitter. This little scroll has long captivated proponents of the entheogen theory of religion, who claim that the main source of human religion is visionary plants such as the *fly agaric* mushroom. The "scroll" that tastes sweet but makes John's stomach bitter is considered by proponents of this theory to be evidence of John

---

[151] See Charles, 239.

partaking of entheogens on Patmos to produce visionary experience.[152]

The angel then commissions John to "prophesy again about many peoples and nations and languages and kings" (10:11). Effectively, this interlude provides a segue from the first reading of the sealed scroll in chapters 6-11, which is rather oblique, to the implied second reading of the scroll in chapters 12-22, symbolized by the open scroll digested by John. Again, the "theory of recapitulation" recognizes that the book is not a sequential narrative in that the second part of Revelation recapitulates the first part. Once the seventh trumpet is blown, the contents of the scroll are revealed, but in a veiled and indirect manner. The pattern unfolds again, though more explicitly, in chapters 12-22. Eating the scroll in chapter 10 provides an interlude which interlocks

---

[152] As Clark Heinrich elaborates: "This 'scroll-eating' [in Revelation] is the same as in Ezekiel, a metaphor for the dried cap of a fly agaric mushroom. Dried caps can be rolled and unrolled like a scroll and have a sweet, honey-like smell, unlike the fresh mushroom, yet eating them often causes an upset stomach. The veil remnants on the cap often look like obscure writing of some kind, while the cap itself contains, and can reveal, the 'word of God', a word that can be seen as well as heard through the secret door of the mind." See Clark Heinrich, *Strange Fruit: Alchemy, Religion and Magical Foods: A Speculative History* (London: Bloomsbury, 1995), 129.

the original with the expanded version of events.[153]

It is crucial to recognize that Revelation's rhetoric of judgment expresses hope for the conversion of nine-tenths of the nations.

The interlude continues by introducing two witnesses in sackcloth with the authority to prophesy for one thousand, two hundred and sixty days (11:1-14).[154] Thought to be metaphors for Israel and Christ, the witnesses are then killed by the beast from the bottomless pit, and after three-and-a-half days raised from the dead. An encouraging anecdote follows: after the witnesses are raised from the dead, they watch from heaven the events surrounding an earthquake in

---

[153] See Adela Yarbro Collins, "The Apocalypse (Revelation)" in *The New Jerome Biblical Commentary*, ed. Raymond Brown, Joseph Fitzmeyer, and Roland Murphy (Englewood Cliffs, NJ: Prentice Hall, 1990), 1007.

[154] "Witness," in Revelation, is another word for "martyr": see vs. 1:5; 2:13; 3:14; and 17:6. "That the beast "makes war on the witnesses in 11:17 as he does on all Christians in 12:17 and 13:7," suggests Murphy "supports the theory that the witnesses represent not two individuals but the prophetic activity of the church." See Murphy, 265.

which nine-tenths of the people of a city are encouraged to repent and give glory to God.

This episode represents a tremendously significant commentary on God's mercy, for as Elizabeth Schussler-Fiorenza recognizes, "It is crucial to recognize that Revelation's rhetoric of judgment expresses hope for the conversion of nine-tenths of the nations in response to Christian witness and preaching; otherwise, one will not understand that the author advocates a theology of justice rather that a theology of hate and resentment."[155] This first cycle of visions closes with the blowing of the seventh trumpet, inspiring rejoicing in heaven and flashes of lightning as the temple opens to reveal the ark of the covenant (11:15-19).

Seven Unnumbered Visions, First Series (12:1-15:4)

In the second half of Revelation, the beast introduced in chapter 11 takes on a primary role as the enemy of God, the Lamb, and the church. Boring argues that the first section in this half,

---

[155] See Schussler Fiorenza, *Vision of a Just World*, 79.

from verses 12:1 - 15:4, "is the central axis in this book and the core of its pictorial argument."[156] This section holds yet another series of seven visions, though this is a less explicit series upon which there is some interpretive disagreement.[157] Scholars have determined that the first of these unnumbered visions is a version of the "combat myth" of the ancient Near East, an influence that pervades the whole book although it is found in its most succinct form in chapter 12.[158]

Chapter 12 tells of a cosmic struggle between "a woman clothed with the sun" and "a great red dragon" (12:1-6; 13-17) that closely parallels the Apollo myth of the dominant Roman culture.[159]

---

[156] Boring, 150.

[157] Different interpreters divide this material differently. Mounce, for example, cannot separate these events into a series of seven; his interpretation generically titles the section 12:1-14:5 as "Conflict Between the Church and the Powers of Evil." See Robert Mounce, *The Book of Revelation* (Grand Rapids: Eerdmans, 1977), 229-281. However, as a convincing division into seven visions is made by Yarbro Collins, this essay will adhere to her interpretation. See Yarbro Collins, *The Combat Myth*, 37-38.

[158] See Ibid., 57.

[159] The first emperor to persecute the Christians, Nero appropriated Apollo imagery for himself. See Murphy, 280.

This image is juxtaposed in an A-B-A ring cycle with an image of war breaking out between the dragon and his demons and Michael and the angels in heaven (12:7-12) that constitutes the first of the unnumbered visions. Representing "the movement from persecution to salvation through combat," this pattern taps into deep archetypes of conflict and resolution evident in the human psyche since ancient times.[160]

The second unnumbered vision (13:1-10) begins when the dragon turns attention toward the inhabitants of the earth. Situating himself on the seashore, the dragon calls a great beast out of the sea, a wounded beast with seven heads and ten horns that is simultaneously like a leopard, a bear, and a lion, uttering blasphemous names. Numerologically, the beast's seven heads and the dragon's seven horns are apparent references to their attempt to usurp the authority of God, while the wound is an obvious allusion to Christ. However, these images originate in Daniel 7, in which four beasts arise from the sea, one like a lion with eagles wings, another like a bear, one

---

[160] Ibid., 56.

like a leopard, and the fourth described as "terrifying," with ten horns and "a mouth speaking arrogantly."[161]

In Revelation 13:4 the people worship the beast, saying "Who is like the beast, and who can fight against it?" Here Ellul uncovers a revealing characterization of the state or empire represented by the beast:

> "Now this power of the state is given to it by the Dragon ... Which is to say that the power of the state is not of the natural, naturalistic, sociological order; it comes from the power of chaos, for the destroyer, as admirably organized and regulated as it is, always expresses chaos."[162]

The beast is analogous to the power of empire; thus it appears that "the inhabitants of the earth" can "find of themselves no higher divinity than

---

[161] "Our author is not interested in tracing a succession of kingdoms," writes Murphy, "rather he concentrates on Daniel's fourth beast and assimilates the other beasts to it." Ibid., 299.

[162] Ellul, 94.

the state and put their hope and faith in it."[163] Revelation thus implies the opposite of that civil religion that finds divine authority in national myths of state or empire.

Here the Apocalypse reveals world-shattering insight into the capacity of empire to captivate human allegiance; as Ellul interprets, "precisely because [the state] expresses a spiritual power, men, who feel it deeply, worship it."[164] This propensity for idolatry is Babylon's sin. "Babylon's futility is her idolatry – her boast of justifying significance in her glory as a nation," claims Stringfellow. "The moral pretenses of Imperial Rome, the millennial claims of Nazism, the anxious insistence that America be "number one" among nations ... all are versions of Babylon's idolatry.[165]

---

[163] Ibid.

[164] Ibid., 95.

[165] Stringfellow, *An Ethic for Christians*, 51. "The American vanity as a nation has, since the origins of America, been Babylonian," writes Stringfellow, "boasting, through Presidents, often through Pharisees within the churches, through folk religion, and in other ways, that America is Jerusalem. This is neither an innocuous nor a benign claim; it is the essence of the doctrine of the Antichrist." Ibid., 114.

Similarly, popular interpretation has long recognized this beast - and also the second beast, the beast of the land - to be a depiction of the coming of the Antichrist as described in 1 John 2:18: "Children, it is the last hour! As you have heard, the antichrist is coming." Specific to John's epistles, the name of antichrist has long been used to describe a character that appears in apocalyptic prophecy since Old Testament times.

The American vanity as a nation, boasting through Presidents and in other ways that American is Jerusalem, is the essence of the doctrine of the Antichrist.

Known as the "man of sin" in the letters of Paul (2 Thess. 2:3), and by the "king of the north" (Dan. 11:40) and other names in the Old Testament, the antichrist is portrayed in Revelation as first a rider on a white horse and then as a beast rising out of the sea. In fact, Revelation 13 describes two beasts - one rising from the sea and one that rises out of the earth - and popular interpreters often argue over which

141

better represents the figure of the Antichrist. Considering that the Antichrist should properly parallel the Christ in terms of his power and authority, it seems more reasonable that the beast of the sea represents the Antichrist, while the beast of the land must represent a lower-level local official acting on behalf of the Antichrist.

A brief exercise in comparison with the "man of sin" from 2 Thess. 2: 3-12 will serve to illustrate that the beast of the sea better represents this figure of prophecy. For instance, the beast of the sea draws his authority directly from the dragon, or Satan (see Rev. 12:18-13:1); while Paul writes that "the coming of the man of sin is apparent in the working of Satan, who uses all power, signs, lying wonders, and every kind of wicked deception" (2 Thess. 2:9-10). Likewise, "in amazement, the whole earth followed the [first] beast"; in fact, they "worshiped the beast, saying, 'Who is like the beast, and who can fight against it" (Rev. 13:3-4)?

The beast is described as having ten horns and seven heads – the same as the dragon - which at that time would likely have been understood as a reference to the Roman emperors. In Revelation chapter 17, an angel interprets "the mystery ... of the beast with seven heads and ten horns" (17:7). "As for the beast that was and is not," interprets the angel, "it is an eighth but it belongs to the seven, and it goes to destruction. And the ten horns that you saw are ten kings who have not yet received a kingdom" (17:11-12).

The physical similarities between the beast of the sea and the dragon serve to emphasize that this beast is a representative of Satan; and the fact that ten kings are attached to him as horns show that he is a great emperor with the power of kings at his command. The beast was "like a leopard, its feet were like a bear's, and its mouth was like a lion's mouth" (13:2), which has given rise to speculation in recent history of the beast's ties to Russia (the bear) or the United Kingdom (the lion).

The unparalleled power and authority of this beast suggest that this is the same one of whom Paul wrote: "Let no one deceive you in any way; for that day will not come unless the rebellion comes first and the lawless one is revealed, the one destined for destruction." Paul was referring to one like the "king of the north" of Daniel's prophecy that stands as ruler of all at the time of the end, and who "shall pitch his tents between the sea and the beautiful holy mountain" (Dan. 11:45).

Actualized to the modern context, this person will appear as one who holds significant political and military power, enough to be in military control of the entire earth. Again, the only contemporary figure that could possibly wield that much power in this generation is the President of the United States, though many anticipate that the Antichrist will be the leader of a coming One World Government.[166] What's more, the beast is "allowed to wage war on the saints and to conquer them" (13:7), which actualized into today's context could be the result of our proposed national health care policy's

---

[166] Like Daniel before him, John prophesies that the kings of the earth "will give their power and authority to the beast" establishing a one world government for the sake of world peace (see Rev. 17:9-13). In 1991, President George H.W. Bush articulated the United States' efforts to establish a one world government when he described the Gulf War as about "more than one small country; it is a big idea; a new world order [for] peaceful settlements of disputes". See Joseph F. Nye, Jr., "What New World Order?" *Foreign Affairs*, Spring 1992.

objective to extend federal abortion funding domestically and internationally (see Rev. 6:11).[167]

All those whose names "have not been written from the foundation of the world in the book of life" (13:8) are destined to worship the beast. The third of the unnumbered visions (13:11-18) is of a beast that arises out of the earth, a beast with two horns like a lamb and speech like a dragon, that "exercises all the authority of the first beast on its behalf, and it makes the world and its inhabitants worship the first beast" (13:12). Furthermore, this beast "deceives the inhabitants of earth, telling them to make an image for the beast ... and it was allowed to give breath to the image of the beast so that the image of the beast could even speak" (13:15).

 These characteristics, according to popular interpretation, describe nothing better than the effect of modern-day television programming:

---

[167] Expanding abortion access is not the only means by which government intervention in medical care can "wage war on the saints." The proposed national health care plan features denying expensive medical care to seniors as a primary means by which to cut costs. See Christian J. Krauthamer, "The Emanuel-Fuchs Voucher Plan for Health System Reform," *American Medical Association Journal of Ethics*, July 2005. Accessed online <https://journalofethics.ama-assn.org/article/emanuel-fuchs-voucher-plan-health-system-reform/2005-07.>

the all-pervasive vehicle for spreading the cultural and consumer message of "America" here and around the world. "Television is the image of the beast" is a familiar billboard advertisement in twenty-first century Sao Paolo, Brazil.[168] Again, these days television's favorite talking head is typically that of President Obama.

"Television is the image of the beast" is a familiar billboard advertisement in twenty-first century Sao Paolo, Brazil.

Perhaps the most remarkable aspect of this beast is that it marks the number of the beast from the sea on everyone's hand or on their forehead: 666. No one will be able to buy or sell without the mark.[169] The development of modern technology for monetary transactions encourages further speculation on this theme in the spirit of actualizing the text. For example, in Mike Leigh's

---

[168] See Kovacs and Rowland, 156.

[169] Yarbro Collins suggests that the reference is to coinage: recalling that in the war of 66-70 C.E. the Zealots refused to carry Roman coins because of their idolatrous imagery. See Adela Yarbro Collins, "The Political Perspective of the Revelation to John," *Journal of Biblical Literature* Vol. 96, No. 2, June 1977, 252-254.

1994 film *Naked*, the protagonist points to the UPC barcode, which he claims has a standard format of six bars with six lines per bar, hypothesizing that the barcode will soon be tattooed on human hands and foreheads to make it easier to make purchases.[170] Others forecast that consumers will have microchips implanted to the same effect.

The fourth unnumbered vision in this series (14:1-5) contrasts with the third in depicting a group that is spared from this tribulation, the 144,000 virgins who have been sealed with the name of the Father and the Son on their foreheads.[171] Schussler Fiorenza warns against a literal reading of virginity here, saying that "since in the rhetorical language and sign system of Revelation sexual language is used metaphorically, the phrase 'they have not soiled themselves with women' refers to the idolatry of

---

[170] *Naked*. Directed by Mike Leigh, starring David Thewlis, Thin Man Films, 1993.

[171] The phrase which allegedly commands wearing *tefillin* appears four times in the Old Testament (Ex. 13,9; Ex. 13,16; Dt. 6,8-9; Dt. 11,18) . In the New Testament, *tefillin* are translated as phylacteries, as in Matt. 23:5: "for they make their phylacteries broad and their fringes wide."

the imperial cult."[172] Yet the concreteness of the description convinces others that literal virginity is meant, as many priests and warriors of that era were often commanded to abstinence.[173] If literal virginity is meant here, it may lend weight to the suggestion that some of these martyrs will be infants killed by abortion (see commentary on Rev. 6:11).

The fifth unnumbered vision is a series of three angels, each with a message for the inhabitants of the earth (14:6-13). The first proclaims the coming judgment, asking all people to give glory to God. The second proclaims "Fallen, fallen is Babylon the great! She has made all nations drink of the wine of the wrath of her fornication" (14:8). The earliest mention of Babylon in Revelation, this message foreshadows the long discourse on Babylon's fall in chapter 17-18.[174] Speaking of contemporary realities as

---

[172] See Schussler Fiorenza, *Vision of a Just World*, 88.

[173] See Adela Yarbro Collins, "Women's History and the Book of Revelation," *Society of Biblical Literature Seminar Papers*, ed. Kent Richards (Atlanta: Scholar's Press, 1987), 86.

[174] "Babylon the great" – in Rev. 14:8; 16:19; 17:5; 18:10, and 18:21 - may derive from Dan. 4:30.

"Babylon" allows Revelation to echo the prophets of old (Isa. 21:9; Jer.51:7), announcing a future event as if it was already past. The third angel predicts punishment for "those who worship the beast and its image, and receive a mark on their foreheads and on their hands" (14:9) promising "torment with fire" and "no rest day and night" (14:10-11).

Another judgment scene, vision six is an eschatological double harvest: a grain harvest (14:14-16); and a grape harvest (14:17-20).[175] The harvest is but another way of describing the punishment readied for those who follow the beast.[176] The seventh, and last, of the unnumbered visions is a scene of the heavenly chorus singing "the song of Moses ... and the

---

[175] This imagery is inspired by Joel 3:13: "Put in the sickle, for the harvest is ripe. Go in, tread, for the wine press is full. The vats overflow, for their wickedness is great."

[176] The blood that flowed from the wine press "as high as a horse's bridle" in vs. 14:20 recalls a scene from another apocalyptic text: "The horse shall walk through the blood of sinners up to his chest; and the chariot shall sink down up to its top" (1 Enoch 100:3).

song of the Lamb" (15:2-4).[177] This last vision interlocks with the next series of seven, the seven bowls, by way of a liturgical interlude (15:1, 5-8).

The Seven Bowls (15:1; 15:5-16:21)

The seven bowls closely parallel the seven trumpets, and both recall the plagues of Exodus. The bowls do not describe a second series of events; rather, they recapitulate the content of the trumpets, intensifying and completing the trumpet's depiction of the plagues. When the angel pours out the first bowl (16:2), it brings painful sores upon all those who have the mark of the beast, recalling the sixth plague of Exodus, the plague of boils. The second angel's bowl turns the sea to blood, destroying all ocean life (16:3), while the third bowl turns the waters of the rivers and springs to blood (16:4-7). The plagues together recall the first Exodus plague, where the water was turned to blood. Bowl number four causes the sun to increase its heat so that the inhabitants of the earth curse God

---

[177] Murphy recognizes that "the specific reference to the song of Moses in the seventh unnumbered vision (15:2-4) prepares the way for the extensive exodus imagery of the bowls." See Murphy, 336.

(16:8-9). The fifth angel's bowl (16:10-11) invokes darkness as does the fifth trumpet, recalling the ninth Exodus plague, yet the people still do not repent.

Bowl six dries up the Euphrates river to open a passage for invaders from the East (16:12-16).[178] Unclean spirits then come from the mouths of the three evil figures: "And I saw three foul spirits like frogs, coming from the mouth of the dragon, from the mouth of the beast, and from the mouth of the false prophet" (16:13).[179] These spirits coming from the mouths of the evil figures are thought to symbolize the propaganda of empire, as the demonic spirits go about performing signs that somehow draw together the kings of the world under their influence (16:14).[180] Actualized

---

[178] Murphy writes that both the sixth trumpet and the sixth bowl "build on the Roman fear of the Parthian empire to the east of the Euphrates." See Murphy, 340.

[179] "Foul spirits" is the same phrase as is usually translated "unclean spirits" in the gospels.

[180] See Mounce, 299. This should be compared to the fact that in 1:16 and 19:15 a sharp sword comes from Christ's mouth. Revelation deals with a clash of claims made by empire and by Christians. "It is a war of words and myths more than weapons." See Murphy, 343.

into today's context, one could imagine these evil figures as representing, say, the government, the media, and the university system – empire's three primary vehicles of propaganda – and the voices emanating from them as these same "foul spirits".

Revelation deals with a clash of claims made by empire and by Christians. It is a war of words and myths more than weapons.

The place where the kings of the earth are to gather offers another fabled image from the Apocalypse: that of Armageddon, or Harmagedon (16:16), the focus of much "decoding" interpretation. Usually spelled Armageddon in English, and the subject of many conflicting interpretations, most scholars today seem to believe that the Hebrew word Harmagedon is a combination of the Hebrew for mountain (*har*) and Megiddo, the site of key Old Testament battles.

For many interpreters, Armageddon is the symbol of the ultimate cataclysm: World War III, for instance, or a nuclear holocaust. Popular interpretation among conservative Protestants today perceives Armageddon to be part of an eschatological scenario that will be soon be enacted: in the last days there will be an increase in apostasy and natural disasters, culminating in the Great Tribulation; then Christ will return to defeat the Antichrist in the battle of Armageddon, restore the temple in Jerusalem, and establish the millennial kingdom.[181]

An odd verse, set apart parenthetically in the NRSV, is 16:15: ("See, I am coming like a thief! Blessed is the one who stays awake and is clothed, not going about naked and exposed to shame.") Such an abrupt statement would seem out of place in almost any other document, but in Revelation it almost seems natural that Christ would directly interject his prophetic pronouncements into the story. Not only does it have the effect of catching the audience's attention, this saying recalls the verse from 2 Peter that teaches: "But the day of the Lord will come like a thief, and then the heavens will pass

---

[181] See Kovacs and Rowland, 175.

away with a loud noise, and the elements will be dissolved with fire, and the earth and everything that is done on it will be disclosed" (2 Pt. 3:10). Effectively, this verse reminds the reader that Jesus could come at any time.

The seventh bowl (16:17-21) is poured out on the air, prompting a voice from the temple to exclaim, "It is done!" Adela Yarbro Collins suggests that this reflects a Hellenistic cosmology recognizing four elements, earth, air, fire, and water: i.e., the first three bowls are directed at the earth and waters, the fourth bowl is poured on the sun, and the seventh bowl is poured on the air. [182] Singled out for God's wrath, Babylon is split apart in an earthquake, while the accompanying hail and thunder recall the seventh Exodus plague. The fact that Babylon is here singled out - "God remembered great Babylon and gave her the wine cup of the fury of his wrath" (16:19) - provides a segue into the next major section of Revelation, what many scholars identify as "the Babylon Appendix."

---

[182] See Adela Yarbro Collins, "The History of Religions Approach to Apocalypticism and the 'Angel of the Waters' (Rev. 16:4-7)," *Catholic Bible Quarterly* 39 (1977), 374.

The Babylon Appendix (17:1-19:10)

The Babylon Appendix (17:1-19:10) contains a vision of Babylon's fall and the reactions to its demise. Chapter 17 depicts Babylon as a woman seated on a scarlet beast, a "great whore" in stark contrast with the image of the church as the virgin bride of Christ in chapters 19 and 21. While this is the first appearance of the whore in the narrative, the city that she represents has already been characterized as the beast and as Babylon.

The image is not unexpected as Revelation has already described unfaithfulness to God as "fornication" (2:20-22; 9:21; 14:8). And while this characterization of Babylon as "whore" may seem very graphic to today's sensibilities, sexual imagery denigrating to women is common in the bible: for example, Ezekiel calls the northern and southern Israelite kingdoms whores unfaithful to God (Ez. 23), and also graphically depicts Jerusalem as an unfaithful wife (Ez. 16).[183]

---

[183] In much the same way, God orders the prophet Hosea to marry a prostitute to symbolize God's marriage to unfaithful Israel. See Mounce, 307-8; also Isa. 1:21; Jer. 2.20-31; 13:27.

The great whore is described as seated on "many waters [that] are peoples and multitudes and nations and languages" (16:15), a suitable image for empire. She is "the one with whom the kings of the earth have committed fornication" (17:2), specifying this chapters' concern with political entities and rulers. Her ostentatious clothing and jewelry indicate the seductiveness of her wealth, and she wears her name, called a "mystery," on her forehead (17:5). In apocalyptic contexts, the name "mystery" refers to insight about the true nature of things available only through revelation.[184] Going by appearances, the people would undoubtedly worship this caricature of empire. But Revelation reveals her true name - "Babylon the great, mother of whores and of earth's abominations" (17:5) - thereby condemning the empire, not only for "fornication," but for being "drunk with the blood of the saints" (17:6).

---

[184] In Revelation, both the followers of the Lamb (7:3; 9:4; 14:1; 22:4) and the followers of the beast (13:16; 14:9; 20:4) wear names on their foreheads signifying whether they belong to the Lamb or the beast. See Murphy, 356.

Chapter 17 provides another terrific temptation for decoders of the apocalypse when it explains the beast's heads and horns by saying, "This calls for a mind that has wisdom" (17:9).[185] The seven heads are said to be seven kings, five of whom "have fallen"; the sixth reigns; and the seventh is yet to come but will "remain only a little while" (17:9-10); while "the beast is an eighth, but it belongs to the seven."

Historical-critical interpreters have created elaborate schemes to connect the seven kings to early Roman emperors: for instance, Aune supplies a chart that outlines eight different ways of doing this. However, popular and actualizing interpreters of biblical prophecy prefer to identify modern rulers such as Hitler, Bush, or Obama to be these kings: i.e. the "eighth" that "belongs to the seven" could represent George W. and H.W. Bush, or Hillary and Bill Clinton. Chapter 17 concludes with a prediction of Babylon's doom.

---

[185] This recalls the similar notice in 13:18 when the name of the beast (666) was divulged.

The heart of the Babylon Appendix (17:1-19:10), Chapter 18 is much more specific about the charges against Babylon than is most of Revelation. In verses 2 and 3 an angel declares: "Fallen, fallen is Babylon the great! It has become a dwelling place of demons. For all the nations have drunk of the wine of the wrath of her fornication, and the kings of the earth have committed fornication with her, and the merchants of the earth have grown rich from the resources of her luxury." The core of Revelation's charges against Babylon can be found here in verse 3 and can be divided into two parts.

Going by appearances, the people would undoubtedly worship this caricature of empire. But Revelation reveals her true name - "Babylon the great, mother of whores".

The initial charge echoes the theme established in chapter 17, condemning Babylon for "fornication" with the kings of the earth and with the nations, those have "drunk of the wine of the wrath of her fornication." Elaborating, the author suggests that Babylon is blameworthy because "the merchants of the earth have grown rich from the resources of her luxury." Chapter 18 continues with the laments of the kings and the merchants and the seafarers - "those astronauts of the epoch"[186] - who grow rich from the trade of goods, including human lives. It then details the mourning of the wealthy, who weep at Babylon's demise, asking "What city was like the great city?" "The fall of Babylon, representing Rome, means disaster for those with a vested interest in the political and economic system at which Rome is the center," writes Murphy. "The ones who mourn Rome's destruction are those who profit from its injustice."[187]

Recalling the dual charge in verse 3 is verse 7, which condemns Babylon because "she glorified herself and lived luxuriously." The reasons for this condemnation are clear, for, as Murphy interprets: "As is true in the real world, economic exploitation and political claims go hand in hand. Because Babylon claims a certain status for

---

[186] Ellul, 200.

[187] Murphy, 375.

herself, a status the seer considers a challenge to God, she confiscates the world's resources to support her own extravagant lifestyle, a lifestyle parodied in the whore."[188]

It appears that Revelation condemns Babylon largely *because* it is rich: "For your merchants were the magnates of the earth and all nations were deceived by your sorcery" (18:23). As Murphy interprets: "The word 'for' or 'because' introduces the reasons for Babylon's punishment. Babylon makes rich the merchants with whom it deals. In the seer's view, this is not because they fulfill legitimate needs but because they cater to Babylon's extravagant and wasteful desires."[189] These wealthy merchants are implicated also in Babylon's deception of the people, or what Revelation calls "sorcery" (18:23).

The human reactions to Babylon's fall in 18:1-19:10 may help us better understand why God judges Babylon. This section contains a

---

[188] Ibid., 371.

[189] See Ibid., 377.

series of angelic announcements and human laments contrasting joy in heaven over the reign of God's justice alongside sorrow from the inhabitants of Babylon that their prosperity is at an end. The concrete claims against Babylon fall into two main categories: economic injustice and the persecution of Christians. In 18:3, an angel condemns Babylon because "the merchants of the earth have grown rich from the power of her luxury." Then a voice from heaven pronounces: "As she glorified herself and lived luxuriously, so give her a like measure of torment and grief" (18:7).

The merchants, "those who gained their wealth from her" (18:15), weep "since no one buys their cargo anymore" (18:11), a cargo of luxury items enumerated in verses 12 and 13, including "slaves - and human lives." While the angels rejoice at God's justice being done, the merchants of Babylon mourn that the "dainties" and the "splendor" of the empire are now gone forever (18:14). The seafaring merchants grieve the empire's destruction as well, asking "what city was like the great city?" (18:18).

In contrast, it is Revelation's claim that from the perspective of the poor and of those persecuted by empire, and consequently that of the angels in heaven, the destruction of Babylon's economic system is something to positively celebrate. Recall how, in Rev. 6:5-6, opening the third seal caused a recognition of how empire's economic policies put terrible pressure on the poor, in that subsistence items like wheat and barley were subject to terrible inflation, while luxury items remained unaffected.

Babylon was also condemned because it persecuted the saints and prophets: verse 18:24 specifies that "in you was found the blood of prophets and of saints and of all who have been slaughtered on earth."[190] In much the same way, Matthew's Jesus says to the scribes and Pharisees, "Therefore I will send you prophets, sages, and scribes, some of whom you will kill and crucify, and some you will flog down in your synagogues and pursue from town to town, so that upon you

---

[190] Schussler Fiorenza considers 18:24 to be "the theological key to the whole Babylon series of judgments" in that the guilt of empire is seen to run so deep that it subsumes the guilt for all murders. See Schussler Fiorenza, *Vision of a Just World*, 95. See also Murphy, 378.

may come all the righteous blood shed on earth" (Mt. 23:34-35).

The saints are advised to "rejoice over her [doom], O heaven, you saints and apostles and prophets, for God has given judgment for you against her ... he has avenged on her the blood of his servants" (18:20, 19:2b). Chapter 19:1-10 is thus an elaborate account of the rejoicing in heaven at the doom of Babylon, in which a great multitude sings, "Hallelujah! The smoke goes up from her forever and ever" (19:3). The appendix closes with an assurance that "these are true words of God" (19:9).

Seven Unnumbered Visions, Second Series (19:11-21:18)

The final series of seven unnumbered visions begins in 19:11 with the Second Coming of Christ. As in his other visions, John does not clearly say that the warrior on a white horse is Christ, rather he says that the rider "is called Faithful and True."[191] The warrior is also called "the Word of

---

[191] In the message to Laodicea, Jesus refers to himself as "the faithful and true witness" (Rev. 3:14).

God" (19:13), a phrase strikingly reminiscent of the gospel of John (1:1, 14). The word is personified as a sharp sword coming out of the riders' mouth, recalling the words of Isaiah: "he made my mouth like a sharp sword."[192]

The saints are advised to "rejoice over her [doom], O heaven, you saints and apostles and prophets, for God has given judgment for you against her" (Rev. 18:20).

The warrior is accompanied by "the armies of heaven, wearing fine linen, white and pure" (19:14): most scholars interpret the armies of heaven to refer to the martyrs. Again, these appear to be the same martyrs that before had cried out for vengeance under heaven's altar, and "were each given a white robe and told to rest a little longer, until the number would be complete ... of their brothers and sisters who were soon to

---

[192] The letter to the Hebrews says that "the word of God is living and active, sharper than any two-edged sword ... it is able to judge the thoughts and intentions of the heart" (Heb. 4:12).

be killed as they themselves had been killed" (see 6:9-11).

The second unnumbered vision is an invitation to a banquet in heaven (19:17-18). It is a grisly feast consisting of "the flesh of kings, the flesh of captains, the flesh of the mighty, the flesh of horses and their riders – flesh of all, both free and slave, both small and great" (19:18). The image is derived from Ezekiel's eschatological battle in chapters 38-39: "you shall eat the flesh of the mighty, and drink the blood of the princes of the earth" (Ezek. 29:18). Even the common and ordinary folk, if guilty of worshipping the beast, will be slaughtered to be served at this gruesome banquet.[193]

Vision number three picks up where the sixth bowl left off, on the plains of Armageddon, with "the beast and the kings of the earth gathered to make war against the rider on the horse and against his army" (19:19-21). The battle is over quickly, as the evil forces are no match for Christ and his martyred army. The beast and the false prophet are thrown into the lake of fire.

---

[193] See Mounce, 347-48.

In the fourth unnumbered vision, Satan himself is bound and thrown into the abyss for a thousand years, "so that he would deceive the nations no more" (20:1-3). This is so Satan will be absent for the coming millennial reign of Christ: "after that," however, "he must be let out for a little while" (20:3). The fifth vision is of the millennial reign of Christ, an earthly kingdom of a thousand years in which the martyrs are vindicated by becoming the rulers of the world.

Apocalyptic interpreters will often identify themselves as either *Premillennialists*, meaning that they believe that Christ will come before the millennium and be present on earth during it; *Postmillennialists*, who believe that Christ will not come until after the thousand year reign of the righteous; or *Amillennialists*, who do not take the earthly millennium literally.[194] Those who reign with Christ during the millennium are a select group, considering that "the rest of the dead did not come to life until after the thousand years

---

[194] "Considering the amount of attention the thousand year reign of Jesus has engendered," writes Murphy, "one might think that it is the most important part of Revelation. Yet it occupies only three verses out of the entire book." See Murphy, 397.

were ended" (20:5). This scenario begs the question of who will be left to be judged during the thousand-year reign.

The sixth unnumbered vision, that of the Last Judgment, is brief and to the point (20:11-15). All the dead, "great and small," stand before the "great white throne" and are "judged according to their works ... and anyone who was not found written in the book of life was thrown into the lake of fire." The author appears eager to reveal the seventh of the unnumbered visions, that of "a new heaven and a new earth" and the initial descent of the New Jerusalem (21:1-8).

The promise of a new heaven and a new earth is an ancient one in Hebrew eschatology. Isaiah has God declare, "I am about to create new heavens and a new earth; the former things shall not be remembered or come to mind" (Isa. 65:17). The promise is a familiar theme of the New Testament as well, as in 2 Peter 3:13: "We wait for a new heavens and a new earth, where righteousness is at home." The vision of the Last Judgement includes a long soliloquy from the throne, one of only two times in the Apocalypse in which God speaks directly.[195] God speaks in covenantal language, emphasizing that "these words are trustworthy and true" (21:5), drawing a stark divide between "the faithless" (21:8) and "those who conquer" (21:7).[196]

The New Jerusalem Appendix (21:9-22:9)

Just as the series of seven bowls in chapter 16 were followed in Revelation's narrative by the Babylon Appendix (17:1-19:10), the final series of seven unnumbered visions (19:11-21:8) is followed by the New Jerusalem Appendix (21:9-22:9). The Babylon Appendix elaborates on the destruction of Babylon in the seventh bowl; likewise, the New Jerusalem Appendix elaborates on the descent of the New Jerusalem in the seventh unnumbered vision. The two appendixes each begin with an invitation made by an angel carrying one of the seven bowls, saying: "Come, I will show you the

---

[195] As in 19:5, this is not God's voice *per se*, but as it issues from the great white throne it carries God's authority.

[196] "See the home of God is among mortals. He will dwell with them; they will be his peoples, and God himself will be with them" (21:3). This is covenantal language, expressing the special relationship between God and Israel (e.g., Lev. 26:11-12; Jer. 31:33; Ezek. 37:27; Zech. 8:8).

judgment of the great whore" (17:1); or, "Come, I will show you the bride, the wife of the Lamb" (21:9). The appendixes also both end in the same way.

"Do not seal up the words of the prophecy of this book, for the time is near" (Rev. 22:10).

The parallelism between the two appendixes highlights the contrast between the great whore and the pure bride, a traditional literary device that symbolizes absolute alternatives by labeling women according to stereotyped categories informed by a patriarchal culture.[197] The New Jerusalem is described as measuring in many multiples of twelve, to symbolize continuity with the tradition of the twelve tribes of Israel and the twelve apostles. This corresponds to Ezekiel's vision of the New Jerusalem, in which each of the four walls has three gates, each one assigned to an Israelite tribe (see Ezek. 58:30-34).

---

[197] Another biblical example of this literary conceit includes the contrast between Folly and Wisdom in Proverbs 8-9.

The city has no temple, as there is no need for a temple when God and the Lamb are there.[198] Likewise, the sun and the moon are unnecessary, "for the glory of God is its light, and its lamp is the Lamb" (21:23). Through the streets of the city flows a river of the water of life, on either side of the river grows the tree of life, and "the leaves of the tree are for the healing of the nations" (22:2). This time it is the angel that pronounces of this prophecy that "these words are trustworthy and true" (22:6).

Epilogue (22:6-21)

The book of Revelation concludes with an epilogue containing a series of prophetic sayings (22:6-21). In contrast with the book of Daniel, where Daniel is told to seal up his revelation until the time of its fulfillment, John is commanded not to seal his revelation, "for the time is near" (22:10). Then Jesus himself appears to personally assert the authenticity of John's testimony (22:16). A final section cautions against tampering with the content of the book (22:18-19),

---

[198] Revelation was written after the temple was destroyed in 70 C.E. See Murphy, 422.

recalling Moses' warning in Deuteronomy 4:3: "You must neither add anything to what I command you nor take anything away from it."

Chanting Down Babylon

Babylon system is the vampire
Sucking the children day by day
Babylon system is the vampire
Sucking the blood of the sufferers
Building church and university
Deceiving the people continually
Me say them graduating thieves
And murderers (look out now)
Sucking the blood of the sufferers
- Bob Marley[199]

Considered to be a "chanting down" of Babylon, traditional reggae music expresses the religion of

---

[199] Bob Marley and the Wailers, "Babylon System," *Survival*, Island, 1979, B00005MKA3.

the Rastafarian people.[200] A Christian/Animist/ Garveyite sect, Rastafarians interpret the book of Revelation to claim that they are the spiritual descendants of Israel/Ethiopia living under the oppressive rule of Babylon.[201] Hence, Rastafarians read the history of colonialism to be an "actualization" of the Babylonian captivity, in which Western civilization constitutes a "succession of oppressive regimes: Persian, Greek, Roman, British, and American."[202] To Rastafarians, "Babylon is an artificial affluent

[200] See Jack A. Johnson-Hill, *I-Sight: The World of Rastafari: An Interpretive Sociological Account of Rastafarian Ethics* (London: The Scarecrow Press, 1995), 257.

[201] In the 1930's, Jamaican native Marcus Garvey's Universal Negro Improvement Association (UNIA) constituted the largest Black movement in the Western Hemisphere. See Johnson-Hill, 16. Garvey's alternative identity politics were formed under such influences as the Ethiopian Baptist Church in Jamaica in which "the Ethiopian throne became a connecting link to the ancient Israelite rulers, and Africa as a primeval homeland." See Johnson-Hill, 14. For Garvey, it was critical that "Blacks consider God in their own terms and not in those dictated by whites." See Elias Farajaje-Jones, *In Search of Zion: The Spiritual Significance of Africa in Black Religious Movements* (Bern: Peter Lang, 1990), 101.

[202] Johnson-Hill, 30. Garvey's UNIA encouraged countless African-Americans to articulate an alternative identity as an oppressed community "who had suffered through four hundred years of the 'Babylonian captivity' of the colonial and post-colonial eras." See Ibid.,17.

society of self-absorbed individuals who worship idols and live decadent lifestyles at the expense of the poor."[203] The celebrated Rastafarian antagonism to "Babylon" is well documented in Marley's "Babylon System," which equates Babylon to a vampire.[204]

A Great Cloud of Witnesses

Although this lucid actualization of Babylon is specific to the Rastafarians of Jamaica,[205] it is part of the inheritance of the larger black community in America, part of a tradition begun in the days of slavery. African-Americans, as aliens in a strange land, adopted the biblical narrative as

---

[203] Ibid., 29.

[204] Marley's interpretation of the "Babylon System" as "the vampire" seems entirely analogous to Stringfellow's view that "America ... is ruled by the power of death." See Stringfellow, *An Ethic for Christians*, 113. In the same way, Stringfellow reports that he would often recognize something familiar in what Karl Barth was articulating. Describing his experience to him, Barth's response was instantaneous: "How could it be otherwise? We read the same Bible, don't we?" See Kellermann, 368.

[205] "Jamaicans," claims Johnson-Hill, are a "culturally hybrid people, neither European nor African." See Johnson-Hill, 12. This was true to a greater degree in Jamaica than the States because "in Jamaica the slaves managed to maintain strong ties to African traditions, perhaps more so than anywhere else in Plantation America." Ibid., 10.

their own, interpreting their experience in light of the stories of Israel's suffering in servitude in Egypt and Babylon and the persecution of the early church. African-Americans, explains Elias Farajaje-Jones, "were welded together by a past from which they had been uprooted, a present in which they were in captivity, and a future in which they were to be freed by the hand of God."[206]

Babylon is an artificial affluent society of self-absorbed individuals who worship idols and live decadent lifestyles at the expense of the poor.

As access to literacy was strictly controlled by the white establishment, black people's awareness of this identity was passed on via oral tradition, and is perhaps best preserved in the sung spirituals of the African-American church. Biblical themes present in these songs are intended to identify the black church as aliens in exile. Some spirituals use specifically apocalyptic themes, for

---

[206] Farajaje-Jones, 34.

example, "Deep River" looks forward to joining in the worship of the elders in Revelation: "Walk into heaven and take my seat / And cast my crown at Jesus' feet."[207]

In similar fashion, "We Shall Overcome" was inspired by Revelation's vision of those who "conquer" by passive resistance; to "conquer" in the modern translation is rendered as "overcome" in the King James Version (Rev. 2:7).[208] These spirituals, and the preaching of the African-American church, enabled many black people to see themselves, not as citizens of America, but as aliens in a strange land.

Only certain subcultures are thoroughly aware of the power of death inherent in the American social purpose, claims Stringfellow: "noticeably those of elderly citizens, of ghettoized blacks, of

---

[207] Kovacs and Rowland, 68. "The African-American spiritual 'In Dat Great Gittin up Mornin' brings together themes from different parts of Revelation," write Kovacs and Rowland, "including the trumpets that unleash plagues (ch.8), the advent of Christ in 19:11-16, the unleashing of Satan (20:7) and the Last Judgment (20:11-15)." See Kovacs and Rowland, 120.

[208] Boring, 61.

prison inmates, of servicemen and Vietnam veterans."[209] In these marginal subcultures, he writes, "the banishment or abandonment of human beings to loneliness, isolation, ostracism, impoverishment, unemployability, separation - all of which are social forms of death - has become so dehumanizing that the victims suffer few illusions about their consignment to death or to these moral equivalents of death by American society."[210] Whereas bourgeois America is enraptured with grandiose visions of national vanity, these subcultures have long been aware of America's true identity.

Stringfellow credits the people of the ghetto with teaching him to recognize how Babylon is made manifest in America.[211] On the streets of Harlem, Stringfellow writes:

[209] Stringfellow, *An Ethic for Christians*, 69.

[210] Ibid.

[211] Beginning in 1956, Stringfellow lived and practiced law in Harlem, of which he said "the street became as much of an office as I ever had." See Kellermann, 44.

Slowly I learned something that folk indigenous to the ghetto know: namely, that the power and purpose of death are incarnated in institutions and structures, procedures and regimes - Consolidated Edison or the Department of Welfare, the Mafia or the police, the Housing Authority or the social work bureaucracy, the hospital system or the banks, liberal philanthropy or corporate real estate speculation. In the wisdom of the people of the East Harlem neighborhood, such principalities are identified as demonic powers because of the relentless and ruthless dehumanization they cause.[212]

The black experience in America is unique in that black people's history has been one of constant subjugation, an experience that bears similarities to the historic circumstances of the early church.

---

[212] Kellermann, 2. Stringfellow's experience was reminiscent of the Apostle Paul's: "though my condition put you to the test, you did not scorn or despise me, but welcomed me" (Gal. 4:14). For example, when Stringfellow first came to Harlem, he reports, it was months before anyone would speak with him. Only when the community saw that he was living as their neighbor in poverty did they open their doors to him. "To practice law in Harlem," he recalls, "it was "essential to become and to be poor." Ibid., 45.

"What is looked upon as an American dream for white people," observed Malcolm X, "has long been an American nightmare for black people."[213]

Sadly, "the American bourgeoisie are nurtured and conformed in a manner that results in a strange and terrible quitting as human beings," explains Stringfellow.[214] "Those who do conform die promptly; they die morally as human beings."[215] Such persons, Stringfellow suggests, are "so much in bondage to the cause of preserving the principality ... that they ... are impaired in the elemental capacity which distinguishes humans from other creatures."[216]

---

[213] Malcolm X gave his legendary "anti-dream" speech in 1962, one year before Martin Luther King's historic speech. See James H. Cone, *Martin and Malcolm in America: A Dream or a Nightmare* (Maryknoll, NY: Orbis Books, 1991), 89. "During the 1950's and 60's," writes James Cone, "no force affected black life as did the ministry of Malcolm X." See Ibid., 91. Malcolm was notorious, as Cone recalls, for "comparing America's coming doom to the downfall and destruction of ancient Egypt and Babylon." Ibid., 158.

[214] Stringfellow, *An Ethic for Christians*, 31.

[215] Kellermann, 51. "The extent to which this society is death-ridden and the culture motivated by the worship of death constitutes relentless pressure on everyone to surrender and conform to that idolatry," continues Stringfellow.

[216] Stringfellow, *An Ethic for Christians*, 30.

They have become "immobilized as human beings by their habitual obeisance to institutions or other principalities as idols."[217]

These are apocalyptic days for America, but an American apocalypse is not likely to be the terminal event in history.

Still, a few white folks are quite well acquainted with America's nightmare. Echoing Malcolm X's prophetic voice, Stringfellow asks: "Is there no American dream except nightmare? If America is Babylon, is there any American hope? The categorical answer is no."[218] Kentucky poet and

---

[217] Ibid. "From such a reign of death – as Saint Paul would have named it – there are by now only such apparent respites or escapes as commercial sports and entertainments, booze, indulgence in nostalgia for a fictional past, a spectator role at moonshots or at heavily staged appearances of the President, the anxious diversions occasioned by inflation and indebtedness, and a place in the audience at officially contrived and sanctioned persecutions of those citizens who are still not conformed." Ibid., 31.

[218] Ibid., 155. Given Malcolm X's tremendous influence on the street, as well as from his pulpit in Harlem's Temple Number Seven, if Stringfellow never heard Malcolm speak, there is little doubt that he would have heard Malcolm X's message repeated in the vernacular of the street. See Cone, 94-95.

farmer Wendell Berry seems to be of the same mind, predicting that: "The earth, and ourselves with it, must certainly be destroyed. This is a time when it is hard, if not impossible, to foresee a future that is not terrifying."[219]

Putting the Fragments Back Together

"These are apocalyptic days for America, I believe," writes Stringfellow, "but an American apocalypse is not likely to be the terminal event in history."[220] To believe this would be to fall victim to an inverse form of the same "American dream" that suggests America is the new Jerusalem. "My concern," claims Stringfellow "is for the exorcism of that vain spirit. My plea is for freedom from this awful naïveté and for healing for this moral flaw. My hope, as a human being, begins in the truth that America is Babylon."[221] Hauerwas offers a similar solution in his certainty that "the story of freedom ... and the institutions

---

[219] Wendell Berry, "The Loss of the Future" in *The Long-Legged House* (New York: Harcourt, 1969), 46.

[220] Stringfellow, *An Ethic for Christians*, 33.

[221] Ibid., 34.

that embody it is the enemy we must attack through Christian preaching."[222] While of the same opinion, Berry speaks a little more gently, suggesting that "We are going to have to gather up the fragments of knowledge and responsibilities [out from under the control of the Babylon system] and put those fragments back together again in our own minds and in our families and households and neighborhoods."[223]

Christian Therapy: Rehabilitating Desire

The Christian tradition claims that human desire has been corrupted by sin, meaning that desire is bent by the world and distorted away from its true object in the worship of God. "For desire to be cured," suggests Miroslav Volf, "one has to learn that none of the objects of this world can

---

[222] Stanley Hauerwas, "Preaching as Though We Had Enemies": cited in Brad J. Kallenberg, *Ethics as Grammar: Changing the Postmodern Subject* (Notre Dame: University of Notre Dame Press, 2001), 139. "Modern individuals," writes Hauerwas, "are a people who believe they should have no story except the story they choose …. Such a story is called the story of freedom and is assumed to be irreversibly institutionalized economically as market capitalism and politically as democracy." Ibid.

[223] Wendell Berry, *A Continuous Harmony: Essays Cultural and Agricultural* (San Diego: Harcourt, 1972), 79.

satisfy human desire because the proper object of human insatiability is the infinite love of God."[224] Hence, Christians must submit their corrupted desire to be transformed by the distinctive therapies of the church; for only by reorienting desire toward its proper concern will the church escape captivity in Babylon.

If Babylon rules by corrupting desire, then Christianity works by curing desire.

Foucault's insight that power is held not by law but by the subtle manipulation of human desire shows Christians how the church might recapture and discipline wayward fragments of desire towards their intended purpose. Recognizing that Babylon operates through redirecting human desire, and comprehending Babylon's influence to be a confluence of technologies that distort desire, Christians are thus able to identify the disciplines of the church to be therapies capable

---

[224] Volf, 268.

183

of recapturing and rehabilitating desire in their own right.

In Bell's analysis "[Babylon] is an ensemble of technologies that disciplines desire according to the logic of production for the market; and no less than [Babylon], Christianity is a material formulation that by means of a host of knowledges, instruments, persons, systems of judgment and spaces assembles desire."[225] If Babylon rules by corrupting desire, then Christianity works by curing desire.[226] Paul alluded to this reality when he wrote, "Do not be conformed to this world, but be transformed by the renewing of your minds" (Rom. 12:2).

What, then, is the therapy that Christianity offers to human desire in the hopes of liberating it from the technologies of Babylon? Foucault's analysis of how the "technology of sex" is "deployed" by the state in the service of "annexing, creating and penetrating bodies" identifies one of the primary

---

[225] Bell, 99. Bell's term, "technologies of desire" connects the "technologies" of Foucault with Deleuze's analysis of "desire" to identify the means by which capitalism governs society. See Ibid., 9.

[226] See Ibid., 44.

mechanisms by which the powers of this world pursue their objective of "controlling populations."[227] Consequently if the "technology of sex" is what conscripts us into the service of Babylon, then as Foucault surmised "it is the agency of sex that we must break away from, if we aim - through a tactical reversal of the various mechanisms of sexuality - to counter the grips of power."[228] In this respect, it is evident that any therapies the church offers to liberate our desire must overcome the hold sex has upon our lives.

Sexuality is an especially dense transfer point for relations of power between an administration and a population.

Commonly dismissed as puritanical, classical Christian therapies for disciplining desire can be a bit more nuanced than is Jesus' famous prescription for combating lust (to gouge out

---

[227] Foucault, *History of Sexuality*, 107. "Sexuality," explains Foucault "is an especially dense transfer point for relations of power between ... an administration and a population ... serving as a point of support for the most varied strategies". Ibid., 103.

[228] Ibid., 157.

one's own eyes).[229] For although Jesus' command is a graphic illustration of just how comprehensive Christian therapies must be in order to liberate desire from the death grip of Babylon, his words are often construed to imply that Christianity demands the elimination of all desire.[230] Yet "Christianity's obsession with subduing desire," as Bell interprets, "is a relatively recent development."[231] Citing Augustine, Aquinas and others, Bell demonstrates that, "prior to the advent of modernity, the end of Christianity was conceived

---

[229] "You have heard that it was said, 'You shall not commit adultery.' But I say to you that everyone who looks at a woman with lust has already committed adultery with her in his heart. If your right eye causes you to sin, tear it out and throw it away; it is better for you to lose one of your members than for your whole body to be thrown into hell" (Mt. 5.27-28).

[230] In truth, the bible offers a variegated portrait of human desire. The author of the letter from James, for example, considers how someone can be "tempted by one's own desire, being lured and enticed by it; [for] when that desire has conceived it gives birth to sin, and that sin, when it is fully grown, gives birth to death" (1:14-15). At the same time, from first to last, the bible celebrates the story of humanity's desire for God: from Moses' desire to see God - "show me your glory, I pray" - on the mountaintop (Ex. 33:18); to early Christians who "desire a better country, that is, a heavenly one" (Heb. 11:16).

[231] Bell, 88.

in terms of the cultivation of a natural desire or passion for God."[232]

Christian Community: The School of Charity

The sermons of Bernard of Clairvaux (1090-1153) emphasize that human desire is a reflection of God's own creative desire. Although "desire has been captured, corrupted and misdirected," Bernard claimed that "the Word has come to heal desire."[233] Monastic life as practiced by Bernard and the Cistercians was about the shaping of virtuous desire. "Far from being a constraint upon nature," writes Michael Casey, "[Cistercian life] works for the liberation of nature from the alien bondage of sin."[234] Cistercian monasteries were no ascetic enclaves, but, ideally, "a school of charity where desire was redeemed."[235]

---

[232] Ibid. The following argument, including the emphasis of this section on Bernard of Clairvaux, owes much to Daniel Bell's *Liberation Theology after the End of History*.

[233] Michael Casey, *A Thirst for God: Spiritual Desire in Bernard of Clairvaux's Sermons on the Song of Songs* (Kalamazoo, MI: Cistercian Publications, 1987), 53.

[234] Ibid., 129.

[235] Bell, 92.

Relevant to this emphasis on rehabilitating desire is the fact that the Cistercian order, like many of the newer monastic orders, recruited adults. Unlike traditional orders, where monks were raised in the cloister almost from infancy, Cistercian recruits came to the monastery after participating in secular adult lives as knights or nobles.[236] Bernard's sermons thus reflect his supervision of monks whose desire had been bent by the world.

Consequently, Cistercian spirituality was not concerned with suppressing desire, but reordering it. For monks under Bernard's care, the monastery offered an assortment of therapies that worked to transform human desire.[237] Disordered impulses of their former lives were intentionally sublimated and reoriented toward spiritual pursuits. "Thus, anger, when controlled, becomes the vehicle of good zeal; pride brought low can be pressed into service in defense of justice," explains Jean Leclercq, and "if

---

[236] Jean Leclercq, *Monks and Love in Twelfth Century France* (Oxford: Clarendon, 1979), 10.

[237] See Bell, 92.

a strong sexuality is brought under control and disciplined by the practice of works of mercy, the very quarter whence people are exposed to the darts of wickedness becomes itself an incitement to solitude for others."[238] Distorted desire, it seems, can be rehabilitated.

Disordered impulses of their former lives were intentionally sublimated and reoriented toward spiritual pursuits.

This doesn't happen overnight. Bernard insists that the healing of desire, by the grace of God, occurs according to a pattern seen in the triad *disciplina / natura / gratia*.[239] Once distortion of desire is recognized, it is first subject to *disciplina*, in which humans respond to grace by forcing themselves to do what is right. The second stage, *natura*, comes only after much practice has led to certain habits of virtuous action. In the third stage, *gratia*, virtue itself is

---

[238] Leclercq, 16-17.

[239] See Casey, 250-251.

one's delight, but this stage is not perfected until the next life.

To effect this transformation involves a vast matrix of therapies. Bernard and his monks lived under the *Rule* of St. Benedict, which counsels a middle way (*via media*), a balanced life of prayer, silence, work, and service.[240] Integral to this task is the liturgy: the focus of monastic life and the primary technology for the reforming of desire.

The ritual imagery and authoritative exegesis of the liturgy, writes Talal Asad, enabled the monks to "redescribe, and therefore in effect reconstruct, their memories in relation to the demands of a new way of life."[241] Liturgy, then, is therapeutic, reconfiguring desire through the

---

[240] The cornerstone of Cistercian life, the *Rule* was written by St. Benedict of Monte Cassino around 530 and still constitutes the basic guide for thousands of monastic Christians to this day. Based on even more ancient orders of discipline, the *Rule* "picks up on the values of the Bible (e.g., prayer, fasting, service of neighbor) and arranges for a life in which these values can be lived out in community." See *The Modern Catholic Encyclopedia*, ed. Michael Glazier (Collegeville, MN: Liturgical Press, 1995), 78-79.

[241] Talal Asad, *Genealogies of Religion: Discipline and Reasons of Power in Christianity and Islam* (Baltimore: Johns Hopkins University Press, 1993), 142.

formation of memory. For example, in sermons, Bernard frequently refers to "the memory of heaven" to describe the nature of eternal life.[242] In so doing, Bernard is redirecting desire away from earthly ambitions towards its true end, the worship of God.

"The entire spectrum of monastic rituals and rites," claims Bell, "from meditation and obedience to manual labor, functioned as [therapies] of desire."[243] Bernard once described the monastery as a "prison with open doors"; for while no one is made to stay, the monastery itself constitutes a therapy by which monks can reform themselves, in which each vow of obedience is about redirecting the will towards a common purpose.[244]

Conceiving of Christianity in terms of redeeming desire does not mandate participation in a cloistered community. Enacting the church's

---

[242] See Casey, 208-230.

[243] Bell, 95.

[244] See Asad, 126.

therapies, however, does require that Christians "place themselves in the types of relations with others and with God that characterize [monastic] life."[245] Unfortunately, living in authentic communal relationship with others is becoming a lost art in an age in which, as Sherry Turkle recognizes, "life is made up of many windows and RL [real life] is only one of them."[246] To practice Christian formation, therefore, it is essential to be intentional in establishing relationships of accountability required for the practice of Christian therapies of desire.

Christian Responsibility: Confronting the Powers

Christians who hope to overcome captivity to the Babylon system must challenge the narrative of propaganda that claims lives in the service of

---

[245] Bell, 97.

[246] Sherry Turkle, *Life on the Screen: Identity in the Age of the Internet* (New York: Simon and Schuster, 1995), 189. Turkle interviews one internet user, typical of many, who spends forty hours a week online, "constructing a life that is more expansive than the one he lives in physical reality." Ibid., 247.

empire.[247] By proclaiming and enacting an alternate story, the church engages in practices that are ultimately of far greater consequence than the state's methods of coercion. The challenge, however, is to take responsibility to continue living according to the church's story even when this clashes with the state's demands. Challenging the dominant narrative in this way requires a paradigm shift so absolute that it needs more than sterile "values": it can only occur through concrete practices in the formative community of the church.[248]

"As human members of Christ's body," observed Barth, "we are able to serve as God's agents to redeem creation by taking human responsibility and dominion over the powers rather than

[247] Described in Rev. 18:23 as the "sorcery" by which "all nations were deceived," the propaganda of empire now piped into people's homes electronically is a difficult narrative to contradict.

[248] "Without considered attention to concrete practices in a church ... political freedom is bereft," writes William Werpehowski. "It is left with a set of Christian 'values' that it would seek to embody in political life; risk[ing] an all too easy Christian accreditation of American democratic institutions." See William Werpehowski, "Reinhold Niebuhr," *Blackwell Companion to Political Theology*, ed. Peter Scott and William T. Cavanaugh, (Malden, MA: Blackwell, 2004), 192.

ceding authority to them."[249] In a story about a
poor Brazilian community confronting
government authorities about the unjust
distribution of milk, Bruce Bradshaw
demonstrates how the church can take
responsibility by calling the powers to account.
Representatives were selected to speak to the
people in power, but:

> In typical fashion, the people in power
> separated themselves from the powers by
> blaming the problem on someone else. (This
> blame perpetuates the idea that the powers
> exist apart from the people in power
> because no one in power takes
> responsibility for the behavior of the
> powers. This reasoning gives the powers an
> autonomous existence).[250]

---

[249] See Willmer, 126.

[250] Bradshaw, 147. In this case, the good news was that
"eventually a public official was influenced to attend a meeting. The
public meeting began, and the people quickly began expressing their
frustrations. After they were done, he said, "Beginning next week, we
will begin distributing the milk tickets. I will keep checking with you
to make sure the milk is reaching the people." Ibid.

This example illustrates how often the powers grow unwieldy precisely because no one takes responsibility for them. Human responsibility, therefore, serves as the instrument of their redemption; for, in this anecdote, "the people, by meeting the powers, redeemed them."[251] "By being trained through Jesus' story," asserts Hauerwas, "we have the means to name and prevent those powers from claiming our lives as their own."[252]

By being trained through Jesus' story we have the means to name and prevent those powers from claiming our lives as their own.

---

[251] Ibid., 148. In this regard, the special circumstance of the modern corporation functioning as an "artificial person" may bear further analysis, for this legal fiction functions to deter human attempts to claim authority over these powers by removing individual culpability for corporate decision-making.

[252] Stanley Hauerwas, *A Community of Character: Towards a Constructive Christian Social Ethic* (Notre Dame: University of Notre Dame Press, 1981), 50.

To Be the Church

Just as the first commandment is to worship God;
the first task of the church, as Hauerwas
acknowledges, is to be the church.[253] "Without
the church the world would have no history,"
claims Hauerwas,[254] and lest he be
misunderstood, R.R. Reno interprets: "Without
the density-conferring work of God in the
identity-forming practices of the church worldly
life is ethereal and weightless."[255] The role of the
church coincides with the first commandment in
Mark 12:29-30: "you shall love the Lord your God

---

[253] To "let the church be the church," a slogan associated with
Hauerwas, "has caught on among those who find the 'social gospel' of
Christian liberalism thin." See Jeffrey Stout, *Democracy and Tradition*
(Princeton: Princeton University Press, 2003), 158.

[254] Stanley Hauerwas, *Christian Existence Today: Essays on
Church, World, and Living in Between* (Durham: Labyrinth, 1998), 61.

[255] "We have political, economic, ethnic, familial
commitments, to be sure," Reno continues, "but the sum of the whole is
less than the parts, and as consequence we have little ballast against the
storms of violence and fear that sweep across our lives. However, if we
are formed by the church ... we have a place to stand against the
supposed "necessities" of life (preservation of one's life, protection of
one's property, defense of one's own kind) that give evil its seeming
cogency and force." See R.R. Reno, "Stanley Hauerwas," *Blackwell
Companion to Political Theology*, ed. Peter Scott and William T.
Cavanaugh (Malden, MA: Blackwell, 2003), 309.

with all your heart, and with all your soul, and with all your mind, and with all your strength."

Secondly, the church has a biblically mandated responsibility to the neighbor which constitutes a mission to the entire human family.[256] However, in witnessing to the secular world in word and action, the church must be careful not to subsume its distinct identity to the project of the nation-state; recognizing, as MacIntyre reminds us, that the "state as a bearer of values always imperils those values."[257] Karl Marx makes similar observations on rights and the state, writing that "if the state is the guarantor of rights, then those rights must be abrogated as soon as they interfere with the security of the state."[258]

---

[256] See the second half of the great commandment in Mark 12:31: "You shall love your neighbor as yourself." A good "neighbor," as defined in Luke 10:25-37, is one who shows mercy to strangers.

[257] Cavanaugh, *Torture and Eucharist*, 195. Inevitably, "as the state itself becomes guarantor of rights," concludes Cavanaugh, "human rights become tied, in bitter irony, to the security of the state." Ibid., 193. For as Cavanaugh interprets: "once the church has been individualized and eliminated as Christ's body in the world, only the state is left to impersonate God."

[258] Ibid., 192.

"The modern nation state is founded on violence" explains Cavanaugh. "If the church is going to resist violence, it has to emerge from its privatization and have a political voice, one that seeks not to regain state power but to speak truthfully about it."[259] Thus, as the very rationale of the state is premised upon the exercise of coercive violence, if the church wishes to serve with integrity it must avoid collaboration with the machinations of empire at all costs.

If the church wishes to serve with integrity it must avoid collaboration with the machinations of empire at all costs.

Status Confessionis

A year after the Nazis came to power in Germany, a group of Christians led by Karl Barth and Dietrich Bonhoeffer, among others, began the "Confessing Church": a movement formed in opposition to the popular "German Christian"

---

[259] William T. Cavanaugh, "Liturgy as Politics: An Interview with William Cavanaugh" *Christian Century*, Dec. 13, 2005, 28.

movement which flew the swastika in their churches and lauded Hitler as the new Messiah who would lead Germany to greatness.[260] Alternatively, the Confessing Church "reject[ed] the false doctrine" of the National Socialist Party, declaring in the Barmen Declaration of 1934 that support for the Nazis violated the basic tenets of the church.[261] "When these alien principles [of National Socialism] are held to be valid," contend the authors of Barmen, "the Church ceases to be the Church."[262] "One had to choose either Christian faith or National Socialism," interprets Robert McAfee Brown. "One could not affirm both."[263]

---

[260] Recalling how German Christians in the 1930's and 40's once affixed the swastika to the center of their Christian crosses and iconography, some churches in the US have been careful not to fly the US flag in too prominent a position in the church sanctuary.

[261] See Barmen Declaration 8.12, in Arthur C. Cochrane, *The Church's Confession Under Hitler* (Philadelphia: Westminster Press, 1962), 237-242.

[262] Barmen Declaration 8.07. See Ibid.

[263] Robert McAfee Brown, "1984: Orwell and Barmen," *Christian Century* Aug. 15, 1984.

A *status confessionis,* or a "confessional situation," is a time in which the church, in view of a particular situation, must affirm the integrity of the gospel without delay.[264] In such a circumstance, it is imperative that the church makes a clear distinction between truth and falsehood, proclaiming the gospel in such a way that no compromise is possible. John Howard Yoder calls this attitude "refusing the identification of the church's mission and the meaning of history with the function of the state in organizing sinful society."[265]

Christians in America are living in a time in which the church can no longer affirm both Christ and "Hitler."

The present state of affairs in the United States seems to demand a movement analogous to the "Confessing Christians" in Nazi Germany. Like the authors of the Barmen Declaration, Christians

---

[264] See Eugene TeSelle, "How Do We Recognize a Status Confessionis?" *Theology Today*, Apr. 1988.

[265] John Howard Yoder, *The Royal Priesthood*, ed. M.G. Cartwright (Grand Rapids: Eerdmanns, 1994), 163.

in America are living in a time in which the church can no longer affirm both Christ and "Hitler." McAfee Brown is surely prescient when he predicts "the formation of an anti-imperial church movement, in which the rejection of America's imperial project is considered a necessary implication of Christian faith."[266] To this end, instead of working to control secular power through indirect influence, the church must claim its own authority in opposition to the authority of the nation-state.[267] Claiming valid authority as the church calls believers to work in the world, but only according to the distinct values and practices of the church. For the church's work is not to petition the state to adopt

---

[266] See McAfee Brown.

[267] Proscribing the temporal relevance of the church through social contract serves to effectively legitimate the authority of the established state; for once the church is sidelined to a "spiritual" function, only the state retains the temporal authority to exercise influence in the world. Accordingly, many political theorists advocate the tight policing of this separation in order that that church and state can fulfill their "proper" function. Yet "at what price," asks Stringfellow, "is this alleged harmony accomplished if in fact the doctrine upon which it rests requires of religious folk a profession, in effect, of atheism?" See William Stringfellow, *A Private and Public Faith* (Eugene, OR: Wipf and Stock, 1999), 30-31.

human rights, but to establish justice as the body of Christ by unmasking the idolatry of the state.

"It is clear in the New Testament," writes Yoder, "that the meaning of history is not what the state will achieve in the way of a progressively more tolerable ordering of society but what the church achieves through evangelism and through the leavening process."[268] The task of the church, therefore, is to share the biblical story and to live according to this story; to be children of God, not representatives of empire; in short, to be the church and not the state.

Corpus Christi[269]

Being the church means that Christians are involved in a community practicing diverse

---

[268] John Howard Yoder, *The Royal Priesthood*, ed. Michael Cartwright (Grand Rapids: Eerdmans, 1994), 163.

[269] In 1981, the US Navy christened a nuclear attack submarine: the *USS Corpus Christi*. Loaded with Tomahawk cruise missiles with nuclear warheads, the subs' motto (each submarine has an individual motto) is "For God and Country." Under protest from the Catholic Church, in 1983 the Navy renamed the submarine *City of Corpus Christi*. See "Christian Soldiers vs. the Navy," *Time*, Dec. 21, 1981.

activities that witness to our authentic identity while denouncing the idolatry of empire. These practices include worship and liturgy, prayer, fasting, and charity, repentance, evangelism, marriage and celibacy, civil disobedience, excommunication, and martyrdom. They are effective because they testify to the truth of the gospel.[270]

Worship and liturgy, including the administration of the sacraments and the proclamation of the word, is the church's "counter-politics" to the politics of empire.[271] As Augustine saw, the liturgy is "true politics" in that it is the public performance of the true eschatological City of God in the midst of another City which is passing

---

[270] It is ironic that, in criticizing Hauerwas, Stout suggests several creative practices by which the church can act as a distinct political body in the world: "[Hauerwas] has advocated neither the withholding of taxes that finance the military, nor participation in costly acts of civil disobedience, nor refusal of communion to soldiers and their commanders." See Stout, 159.

[271] This proposition is derived from Cavanaugh's claim that "the Eucharist is the church's 'counter-politics' to the politics of torture." Explains Cavanaugh: "While torture is an anti-liturgy for the realization of the state's power on the bodies of others, Eucharist is the liturgical realization of Christ's suffering and redemptive body in the bodies of his followers." See Cavanaugh, *Torture and Eucharist*, 205.

away.[272] The Book of Revelation more than any other provides a counter-narrative to the pretense of empire in which the story of the church is told as counter-propaganda to empire's dominant narrative.

The practice of prayer is paramount in that it points the church toward God's purposes, professing that the coming reign is in God's plan and not by human design. Whenever the church is confronted by the world's anxieties, prayer reminds the church of its eschatological orientation. As Barth discovered of the first stanzas of the Lord's Prayer, "the one who prays to the Father cannot but look for the kingdom to come."[273] Moreover, prayer is intrinsically connected to fasting and charity, each contributing to the other like the three legs of a tripod.

The discipline of fasting, part of a traditional Jewish emphasis on prayer, fasting, and charity, has been all but abandoned by the Western

---

[272] Ibid., 14.

[273] See Willmer, 133.

church.[274] Well-attested in the Old Testament,[275] in the New Testament fasting is not commanded, but assumed: when Jesus spoke about fasting, he didn't say if you fast, but "when you fast" (Matthew 6:16).

Liturgy is "true politics" in that it is the public performance of the true eschatological City of God in the midst of another City which is passing away.

Sadly, this discipline is absent from the lives of many Christians today. Yet fasting is Christianity's forgotten therapy for conquering corrupted desire. As Foucault explains:

> Fasting as a way of conquering greed and suppressing fornication is the first link in the causal chain [of] conquering vice. There is a

---

[274] Fasting remains a practice of many Orthodox Christians, Jews, and others. One of the five pillars of Islam (faith, prayer, charity, fasting and pilgrimage) it is a vital tradition for Muslims as well.

[275] Some OT examples of fasting: Ex. 34:28; Deut. 9:9,18; 2 Sam. 12:16,17; Jonah 3:5; Ezra 8:21-23; 10:6; Neh. 1:4; Es. 4:16; Job 33:19,20; Ps. 69:10; 102:4; Is. 58:6; Dan. 9:3,20-23; 10:3; and Joel 2:15.

causal link that binds the [vices] all together. It begins with greed, which ... inflames the spirit of fornication ... which in turn leads to rivalries, quarrelling, and wrath. ... Such a progression implies that one will never be able to conquer a vice unless one can conquer the one on which it leans.[276]

Early Christians would fast in a spirit of prayer and give the money saved from fasting to the needy.[277] Although the biblical model is one of fasting from food, in a consumer society one can fast from many things: fasting from shopping, for instance, in order to give to the poor; or fasting from television so as to make time for prayer and bible study.

---

[276] Michel Foucault, "The Battle for Chastity," in *Michel Foucault: Politics, Philosophy, Future*, ed. Lawrence D. Kritzman (New York: Routledge, 1988), 229.

[277] *The Third Book of Hermas*, or *Similitudes* (100-160 C.E.) records instructions requiring those who fast to pray for purity and to contribute the money saved from fasting to the poor. "This fast ... is exceeding good," instructs an angel. "Therefore keep it. First of all ... keep yourself from every shameful act ... purify your mind ... and computing the quantity of food which you are accustomed to eat ... lay aside the expense which you would have made ... and give it to the widow, the fatherless, and the poor" (5:28-30) [online posting].

The giving of charity, the third leg of the tripod, is also expressly commanded in scripture. From love of neighbor as one's self (Lev. 19:18) to care of the poor (Deut. 15:4) to doing unto others (Mt. 7:12), the bible is concerned with those less fortunate, particularly widows and orphans and sojourners (Lev. 24:19-21).

Perhaps the most convincing depiction of why Christians give charity is found in the parable of the sheep and the goats (Mt. 25:31-46): in which those who give food to the hungry, drink to the thirsty, welcome to the stranger, clothes to the naked, care to the sick, and encouragement to the imprisoned inherit eternal life. Those who do not give inherit eternal damnation.

Repentance is necessary for Christians who have collaborated with the nation-state in violence and injustice.[278] "Christians can atone for their

---

[278] "If it is tempting to suppose that remote proximity abolishes responsibility for the killing," warns Stringfellow, "it must be remembered that the use of apparently anonymous automated weapons exposes the common and equal culpability for slaughter of those who pull the trigger and those who press the button with those who manufacture the means and those who pay the taxes." See Stringfellow, *An Ethic for Christians*, 73.

complicity with violence in the past by refusing to be complicit with state violence now" concludes Cavanaugh.[279] Repentance can also include making direct reparation for sin: for example, Barth taught that the church should accept communist appropriations as penance for past misdeeds.[280]

Evangelism is the call made upon the church in the Great Commission, when Jesus said to his disciples after his resurrection: "Go therefore and make disciples of all nations" (Mt. 28:18-20). Evangelism is the church's mandate to go out into the world. Evangelism is not necessarily verbal; instead, as Stringfellow construes it, "evangelism consists of loving another human being in a way which represents to him the care of God for his

---

[279] Cavanaugh, *Christian Century*, 28.

[280] As Willmer construes, "After 1945, like his Czech colleague J. Hromadka, Barth thought Christians should accept communist appropriations as an historical penitence." See Willmer, 126.

particular life."[281] Evangelism is thus an act of radical welcome, transcending the boundaries of "all nations," in a politics quite different from the politics of the world.

The vocation of marriage, or a similar relational commitment, is another key therapy that the church offers to heal distorted desire. "In an era of aggrandizement ... personal well-being seems to require marking off a boundary of privacy from the welter of public compulsions," writes Nancy Cott. "Marriage can be imagined as setting this boundary and providing private liberty inside it."[282] Not only does living as a married couple or in a monogamous commitment prove

---

[281] Stringfellow, *Public and Private Faith*, 54. "Evangelism," elaborates Stringfellow, "is the event in which a Christian confronts another [person] in a way which assures the other ... that the new life which he observes in the Christian is vouchsafed for him also." See Ibid.

[282] Nancy F. Cott, *Public Vows: A History of Marriage and the Nation* (Cambridge: Harvard University Press, 2000), 226. Cott recognizes that marriage itself has been utilized by economic forces in the state's process of normalization; however, "marriage more recently and paradoxically signifies freedom in a chosen space – a zone marked off from the rest of the world." Ibid.

best for children,[283] it provides a context for disciplining desire towards the worship of God along with strength for the journey.[284]

Marriage ... paradoxically signifies freedom in a chosen space - a zone marked off from the rest of the world.

However unpopular, *celibacy*, observed within a Christian community of support and accountability, is a vocation highly recommended by the ancient church. Students of Revelation may recall the "new song [that] no one could learn ... except those who have not defiled themselves with women, for they are

---

[283] See Sarah McLanahan and Gary Sandefur, *Growing Up With a Single Parent: What Hurts, What Helps* (Cambridge: Harvard University Press, 2006), 45-60.

[284] "Everything you hear in ads and entertainment is telling you that your goal is to wake up next to someone gorgeous tomorrow morning," writes Fredrica Mathewes-Green. "That's the rationale of consumer sex. But I think what humans really want is to wake up next to someone kind, fifty years from tomorrow morning. ... If I get old and cranky, if I get breast cancer, if I get Alzheimer's, he'll stick with me, and I won't be alone, and I'll do the same for him. In this way we show the presence of God to each other, and grow into his likeness." See Frederica Mathewes-Green "Bodies of Evidence," *Touchstone*, June 2005.

virgins" (Rev. 14:3-4). Yet while this promise alone might inspire some to abstain from sex, there is much else in the biblical witness to commend celibacy.[285] Paul commends celibacy above marriage, though "it is better to marry than to burn with passion" (I Cor. 7:8). Jesus also encourages celibacy, advocating for those "who have made themselves eunuchs for the sake of the kingdom of God" (Mt. 19:12), a euphemism that may well describe people called to lives of celibacy.

Civil disobedience, which is at least as old as the Hebrew midwives' defiance of Pharaoh in Exodus 1:19, is sometimes necessary in order to confront the powers, or, in Thoreau's words, to "stop the machine."[286] Conscientious objection is but one of the means of civil disobedience by which the

---

[285] The entire chapter of 1 Corinthians 7 advocates for celibacy. For example, in 1 Cor. 7:32-34, Paul explains his rationale for advocating celibacy, saying: "I want you to be free from anxieties. The unmarried man is anxious about the affairs of the Lord, how to please the Lord; but the married man is anxious about the affairs of the world, how to please his wife, and his interests are divided."

[286] "Let your life be a counter-friction to stop the machine." See Henry David Thoreau, "Civil Disobedience" in *The Portable Thoreau* ed. Carl Bode (New York: Penguin, 1947), 120.

church can disentangle itself from the state, though arguably the most important one. As Cavanaugh advises, "the churches should not defer to the president the decision on what constitutes a just war and what does not. If the church decides that a war is unjust, Christians should refuse to fight it."[287]

Let your life be a counter-friction to stop the machine.

By withholding taxes that sponsor the violence of the state, penitent Christians can refuse being made complicit in empire's atrocities. This and other acts of civil disobedience - nonviolent by definition - have as their premise that to be obedient to God is to refuse complicity with illegitimate authority: "The purpose of the sit-ins," explains Yoder, "is not to coerce the 'adversary' but to communicate to him, to 'get through to him'; the boycott is not a weapon but a refusal to cooperate with wrong practices; the

---

[287] Cavanaugh, *Christian Century*, 30. Pacifists, obviously, would argue that all war is unjust.

'demonstrations' are just that: efforts to point people's awareness to moral issues."[288]

Excommunication, in particular the withholding of communion, was traditionally used by the church to discipline malevolent government authorities.[289] For example, when the emperor Theodosius' troops massacred civilians in Thessalonica, Bishop Ambrose refused the emperor communion until he made public penance in the streets of Milan.[290] Thomas Aquinas formalized this position, teaching that "the church has the authority to excommunicate rulers and absolve their subjects from obedience to them."[291] The ban on communion has since been used as the discipline of last resort, from

------

[288] John Howard Yoder, *For the Nations* (Grand Rapids: Eerdmans, 1997), 101.

[289] "Excommunication (Lat. *ex*, out of, and *communicatio*, communion – exclusion from the communion), the principal and severest censure, is a medicinal, spiritual penalty that deprives the guilty Christian of all participation in ecclesiastical society." See "Excommunication," *Catholic Encyclopedia* [online posting].

[290] Williston Walker, *A History of the Christian Church*, 4th ed. (New York: Scribner, 1985), 160.

[291] Cavanaugh, *Torture and Eucharist*, 196.

Calvin's correction of wayward church members to Romero's calling criminal elites to account.[292]

More recently, the potential impact of this practice could be recognized in a public letter by poet Sharon Olds to First Lady Laura Bush rejecting her invitation to the National Book Festival of September 2005. "Dear Mrs. Bush," she writes:

> I am writing to let you know why I am not able to accept your kind invitation. ... I tried to see my way clear to attend the festival in order to bear witness ... against this undeclared and devastating war. But I could not face the idea of breaking bread with you. What kept coming to the fore of my mind is that I would be taking food from the hand of the First Lady who represents the Administration that unleashed this war and

---

[292] Reports in 2004 of democratic presidential candidate John Kerry's excommunication - supposedly in response to his "pro-choice" position on abortion – have been widely debunked as an urban legend, though one heavily promoted throughout the 2004 election cycle. See Cindy Wooden, "Vatican denies it responded to lawyer seeking Kerry's excommunication," *Catholic News Service*, Oct. 19, 2004 [online posting].

wills its continuation. ... I thought of the clean linens at your table, the shining knives and the flames of the candles, and I could not stomach it. Sincerely, Sharon Olds[293]

Olds' revulsion at sitting at table with this representative of empire is in the spirit of the church's practice of excommunication and illustrates that the church does not require an established disciplinary framework in order to issue such a ban. Indeed, there is nothing to prohibit churches in the United States from shaking off the constraints of civil religion and making a public witness by refusing communion to American government officials.

A martyr is one who lives imaginatively as if death does not exist.

Martyrdom is the church's ultimate witness to God's victory over the unjust power structures of the world. "A martyr is one who lives imaginatively as if death does not exist," writes

---

[293] Sharon Olds, "No Thanks, Mrs. Bush" *The Nation,* Oct. 10, 2005, 5.

Cavanaugh.[294] Based on his reading of Revelation 5, Yoder envisions a new politics in which "the cross and not the sword determines the meaning of history":

> This conception of participation in the character of God's struggle with a rebellious world, which early Quakerism referred to as "the war of the lamb," has the peculiar disadvantage - or advantage, depending on one's point of view - of being meaningful only if Christ be he who Christians claim him to be, the Master. Almost every other kind of ethical approach espoused by Christians, pacifist or otherwise, will continue to make sense to the non-Christian as well[295]

---

[294] Cavanaugh, *Torture and Eucharist*, 65. As Cavanaugh stresses, "The dangerous memory associated with the body of a martyr - preeminently located in the Eucharist – is what forms and identifies a community as the body of Christ in ongoing conflict with worldly power." Ibid., 68.

[295] John Howard Yoder, *The Politics of Jesus* (Grand Rapids: Eerdmans, 1972), 237. "The point is not that one can attain all of one's legitimate ends without using violent means," explains Yoder. "It is rather that our readiness to renounce our legitimate ends whenever they cannot be attained by legitimate means itself constitutes our participation in the triumphant suffering of the Lamb." See Ibid.

Martyrdom does not depend upon the intention of the person killed - "for then indeed," as Cavanaugh discerns, "only God would be able to judge - but whether or not those with eyes to see are able to discern the body of Christ, crucified and glorified, in the body broken by the violence of the world."[296] The witness of Christian martyrdom, therefore, demands recognition by the church, a body of people who see through the biblical lens.

---

[296] Cavanaugh, *Torture and Eucharist*, 64. "It is not the heroism of the individual which is most significant, but rather the naming of the martyr by those who recognize Christ in the martyr's life and death." See Ibid.

Conclusion

The one who testifies to these things says, "Surely I am coming soon!" Amen. Come, Lord Jesus! - Revelation 22:20

Revelation's parable of Babylon provides an alternative to empire's propaganda: a narrative that discloses the apocalyptic reality of our time. Current biblical scholarship establishes that Revelation must always be read according to its original context under the oppression of empire and that a text must be "actualized" (rather than "decoded") so as to allow for the possibility of other interpretations. Utilizing this hermeneutic allows for Revelation's Babylon to be "actualized" in this era as the United States of America.

Today the most pervasive empire the world has ever seen dominates the globe, making unprecedented claims of authority and demanding allegiance from all the peoples of the world by force of arms. Under the circumstances, it is difficult to read the book of Revelation without recognizing an overwhelming analogy between the current state of affairs and the critique of empire found in the biblical witness.

One can discern and identify maturity, conscience, and paradoxically, freedom only among those who are in conflict with the established order.

As the Apocalypse was written to a church under the persecution of empire, it only stands to reason that the most valid interpretation of Revelation must come, not from empire's official guild of scholars, but from church communities that are actively oppressed by empire. "One can discern and identify maturity, conscience, and paradoxically, freedom in human beings," explains Stringfellow, "only among those who are in conflict with the established order."[297]

Concerned with disciplining desire - the constitutive aspect of the human being – towards the service of God, the early church anticipated Foucault in recognizing desire as the very power that motivates reality. Desire is "omnipresent everywhere," explains Foucault, "because it comes from everywhere."[298] When the state exercises power, it does so because it manages to capture existing forces of desire; consequently, it is essential that Christians submit their corrupted desire to be transformed by the distinctive therapies of the church. Foucault's analysis of desire, therefore, helps Christians to discern how the church might recapture and discipline human desire towards its intended purpose.

Hope, then, begins in the ability to reject the "American dream" in favor of a new ethic for

---

[297] See Stringfellow, *An Ethic for Christians*, 31.

[298] Foucault, *History of Sexuality*, 93.

living, a new narrative of existence that transcends America's bondage to death. Hope is found in telling an alternative story: in "promoting new forms of subjectivity through refusal to the kind of individuality which has been imposed on us," as Foucault would say.[299] Hope is found in singing a new song: in "chanting down" Babylon as the Rastafarians do. For though the Babylon system dominates the world, it is the Christian church, through its distinct disciplines and practices, that can offer release from the domination of these powers, just as the church has always promised salvation from sin.

As the psalmist asked during the Babylonian captivity, "How shall we sing the Lord's song in a strange land?"[300] "The answer," responds Stringfellow, "is heard in the jubilation of the heavenly chorus at the doom of Babylon."[301] "Hallelujah!" they sing. "Hallelujah! The smoke

---

[299] Foucault, *The Subject and Power*, 216.

[300] See Psalm 137:1a, 4,

[301] Stringfellow, *An Ethic for Christians*, 156. See also Ibid., 26.

[of Babylon] goes up forever and ever" (Rev. 19:3).

Selected Bibliography

Ahmed, Leila. *Women and Gender in Islam: Historical Roots of a Modern Debate*. New Haven: Yale University Press, 1993.

Alberts, Sheldon. "Chavez uses petro-dollars to help the poor in America." *CanWest News Service*, Dec. 5, 2006. Accessed Dec. 5, 2006 <http://www.commondreams.org/headlines06/1207-06.htm.>

Alter, Alezandra. "For some evangelicals, Mideast war stirs hope." *Miami Herald*, August 8, 2006.

Althaus, Paul. *The Theology of Martin Luther*. Philadelphia: Fortress, 1966.

Asad, Talal. *Genealogies of Religion: Discipline and Reasons of Power in Christianity and Islam*. Baltimore: Johns Hopkins University Press, 1993.

Augustine. *Confessions*, trans. Henry Chadwick. Oxford: Oxford University Press, 1992.

Bacevich, Andrew J. *American Empire: The Realities and Consequences of U.S. Diplomacy*. Cambridge: Harvard University Press, 2002.

Barth, Karl. *Church and State*. London: SCM, 1939.

_____. *Evangelical Theology*. Grand Rapids: Wm. B. Eerdmans, 1963.

Batto, Bernard. *Slaying the Dragon: Mythmaking in the Biblical Tradition*. Louisville: Westminster John Knox, 1992.

Bay, David. "Economic Babylon of Revelation 18 May Be America." *The Cutting Edge* [radio program] aired on August 22, 1992. Accessed December 7, 2005 <http://www.cuttingedge.org/ce1038.html.>

Beatus of Liebana. *Commentary on the Apocalypse*, ed. H.A. Sanders. Rome: American Academy, 1930.

Beard, Charles. "Giddy Minds and Foreign Quarrels (1939)." In Gore Vidal, "We Are the Patriots." *The Nation*, June 2, 2003.

Bell, Jr., Daniel M. *Liberation Theology after the End of History*. London: Routledge, 2001.

Berger, Rose Marie and James Ferguson. "Mind the Gap." *Sojourners*, Dec. 2005: 10.

Berry, Wendell. *A Continuous Harmony: Essays Cultural and Agricultural*. San Diego: Harcourt, 1972.

_____. "The Loss of the Future." In *The Long-Legged House*. New York: Harcourt, 1969: 46-65.

Bonino, Jose Miguez. *Toward a Christian Political Ethics.* Philadelphia: Fortress, 1983.

Boot, Max. "What Next? The Foreign Policy Agenda beyond Iraq." *Weekly Standard,* May 5, 2003.

Boring, Eugene. *Revelation.* Louisville, KY: John Knox Press, 1989.

Bradshaw, Bruce. *Bridging the Gap: Evangelism, Development, and Shalom.* Monrovia, CA: World Vision International, 1993.

Brook, Wes Howard and Anthony Gwyther. *Unveiling Empire: Reading Revelation Then and Now.* New York: Orbis, 1999.

Brown, Robert McAfee. "1984: Orwell and Barmen." *Christian Century,* Aug. 15, 1984.

Burtchaell, James Tunstead. *Rachel Weeping and other essays on abortion.* Toronto: Life Cycle Books, 1982.

Caird, George B. *The Revelation of St. John the Divine.* London: Andam and Charles Black, 1966.

Calvin, John. *Commentary on a Harmony of the Evangelists, Matthew, Mark, and Luke. Vol.3,* tr. William Pringle. Grand Rapids: Eerdmans, 1949.

Cavanaugh, William T. "Liturgy as Politics: An Interview with William Cavanaugh." *Christian Century*, Dec. 13, 2005: 28-34.

_____. *Torture and Eucharist: Theology, Politics, and the Body of Christ*. Malden, MA: Blackwell, 1998.

Casey, Michael. *A Thirst for God: Spiritual Desire in Bernard of Clairvaux's Sermons on the Song of Songs*. Kalamazoo, MI: Cistercian Publications, 1987.

Charles, R.H. *A Critical and Exegetical Commentary on the Revelation of St. John. Vol.1*. Edinburgh: T. and T. Clark, 1920.

Chomsky, Noam. "Promoting Democracy in the Middle East." *Khaleej Times*, Mar. 6, 2005. Accessed Nov. 3, 2006 <http://www.countercurrents.org/iraq-chomsky060305.htm.>

Chopra, Deepak. "The Seduction of Apocalypse." *Huffington Post*, Apr. 7, 2006. Accessed Nov. 15, 2006 < http://www.huffingtonpost.com/deepak-chopra/the-seduction-of-apocalyp_b_18671.htm.>

"Christian Soldiers vs. the Navy," *Time*, Dec. 21, 1981. Accessed March 10, 2006 <http://www.time.com/time/magazine/article/0,9171,925143,00.html?iid=chix-sphere.>

Cochrane, Arthur C. *The Church's Confession Under Hitler*. Philadelphia: Westminster Press, 1962.

Cohen, Shoshanah and Joseph Roussel. *Strategic Supply Chain Management: The 5 Disciplines for Top Performance.* Columbus, OH: McGraw-Hill, 2004.

Cohn, Norman. *The Pursuit of the Millennium.* London: Paladin, 1957.

Collins, Adela Yarbro. *The Apocalypse.* Wilmington, DE: Michael Glazier, 1979.

_____. "The Apocalypse (Revelation)." *New Jerome Biblical Commentary,* ed. Raymond Brown, Joseph Fitzmeyer, and Roland Murphy. Englewood Cliffs, NJ: Prentice Hall, 1990.

_____. *The Combat Myth in the Book of Revelation.* Missoula, MT: Scholar's Press, 1976.

_____. *Cosmology and Eschatology in Jewish and Christian Apocalypticism.* Leiden: Brill, 1996.

_____, ed. "Early Christian Apocalypticism: Genre and Social Setting." *Semia 36: An Experimental Journal for Biblical Criticism.* Atlanta: Scholar's Press, 1986.

_____. "The History of Religions Approach to Apocalypticism and the 'Angel of the Waters' (Rev. 16:4-7)." *Catholic Bible Quarterly* 39 (1977).

_____. "The Political Perspective of the Revelation to John." *Journal of Biblical Literature* Vol.96, No.2, June 1977: 252-254.

_____. "Women's History and the Book of Revelation," *Society of Biblical Literature Seminar Papers*, ed. Kent Richards. Atlanta: Scholar's Press, 1987.

Collins, John J. *The Bible after Babel: Historical Criticism in a Postmodern Age*. Grand Rapids: Eerdmans, 2005.

Cone, James H. *Martin and Malcolm in America: A Dream or a Nightmare*. Maryknoll, NY: Orbis Books, 1991.

Cooper, Helene. "Iran Who? Venezuela Takes the Lead in a Battle of Anti-U.S. Sound Bites." *New York Times*, September 21, 2006.

Cott, Nancy F. *Public Vows: A History of Marriage and the Nation*. Cambridge: Harvard University Press, 2000.

Daniel, E. Rudolph. "Joachim of Fiore: Patterns of History in the Apocalypse." *The Apocalypse in the Middle Ages*, ed. Richard K. Emmerson, and Bernard McGinn. Ithica: Cornell University Press, 1993: 72-88.

Deleuze, Gilles. *Foucault*, trans. Sean Hand. London: The Athlone Press, 1988.

de Tocqueville, Alexis. *Democracy in America*. New York: Harper Perennial, 1988.

D'Souza, Dinesh. "In Praise of American Empire." *Christian Science Monitor*, April 26, 2002.

Dylan, Bob. "Gotta Serve Somebody." *Slow Train Coming*. Special Rider Music (1979) 16932.

Eisenhower, Dwight D. *Public Papers of the Presidents of the United States, 1960-61*. Washington, DC: National Archives of the US, 1961.

Ellul, Jacques. *Apocalypse: The Book of Revelation*. New York: Seabury Press, 1977.

Engdahl, William. *A Century of War: Anglo-American Oil Politics* and the New World Order. Ann Arbor, MI: Pluto Press, 2004.

"Excommunication." *Catholic Encyclopedia* [online posting]. Accessed Apr. 28, 2006 <http://www.newadvent.org/cathen/05678a.htm.>

Farajaje-Jones, Elias. *In Search of Zion: The Spiritual Significance of Africa in Black Religious Movements*. Bern: Peter Lang, 1990.

Farnham, Marynia. *Modern Woman: The Lost Sex*. New York: Harper, 1948.

Firth, Katherine R. *The Apocalyptic Tradition in Reformation Britain 1530-1645*. Oxford: Oxford University Press, 1979.

Foucault, Michel. "The Battle for Chastity." *Michel Foucault: Politics, Philosophy, Future,* ed. Lawrence D. Kritzman. New York: Routledge, 1988: 229-236.

_____. *Discipline and Punish: The Birth of the Prison*, trans. Alan Sheridan. New York: Random House, 1977.

_____. *The History of Sexuality: An Introduction*. New York: Random House, 1978.

_____. "Human Nature: Justice versus Power." *Reflexive Water: The Basic Concerns of Mankind*, ed. Fons Elders. London: Souvenir Press, 1974): 171-184.

_____. "Interview with Michel Foucault." *Power*, ed. J. Faubion, trans. Robert Hurley et al. New York: New Press, 1980: 288-314.

_____. "Naissance de la biopolitique, Cours au Collège de France, 1978-1979." Paris: Gallimard, 2004.

_____. *Power/Knowledge: Selected Interviews and Other Writings 1972-1977*, ed. Colin Gordon. New York: Pantheon, 1980.

_____. "The Subject and Power." *Michel Foucault: Beyond Structuralism and Hermeneutics*, eds. Hubert Dreyfus and Paul Rabinow. Chicago: University of Chicago Press, 1982: 216-223.

_____. "Truth and Subjectivity: the Stoic Practice of Self-Examination." *The Politics of Truth*, eds. Sylvere Lotringer and Lysa Hochroth. New York: Semiottext(e), 1997: 211-227.

Fourth Assessment Report of the Intergovernmental Panel on Climate Change. April 6, 2007. Accessed May 3, 2007 <http://www.ipcc.ch/SPM6avr07.pdf.>

Freeman, Mary Jane. "UNDP Report: A Needless Decade of Despair: Developing Nations Are Dying." *Executive Intelligence Review*, Aug. 1, 2003.

Fukayama, Francis. "The End of History and the Last Man." New York: Avon Books, 1992.

Garrett, Susan R. "Revelation." *Women's Bible Commentary*, eds. Carol A. Newsom and Sharon R. Ringe. Louisville: Westminster John Knox, 1992: 469-474.

"The Georgia Guidestones" [online posting]. Accessed Feb. 3, 2007 <http://www.radioliberty.com/stones.htm.>

Glazier, Michael, ed. *The Modern Catholic Encyclopedia.* Collegeville, MN: Liturgical Press, 1995.

Goldberg, Michelle. *Kingdom Coming: The Rise of Christian Nationalism.* New York: W.W. Norton, 2007.

Gonzales, Justo. *The Story of Christianity: The Reformation to the Present Day.* Peabody, MA: Prince Press, 1999, 256.

Gutierrez, Gustavo. *The Power of the Poor in History*, trans. Robert R. Barr. Maryknoll, NY: Orbis Books, 1983.

Hardell, Lennart, et al. "Tumour risk associated with use of cellular telephones or cordless desktop telephones." *World Journal of Surgical Oncology,* Oct. 11, 2006. Accessed Jan. 9, 2007 <https://www.ncbi.nlm.nih.gov/pmc/articles/PMC1621063/.>

Hassan, Ghali. "How the US Erase Women's Rights in Iraq." Global Research [online posting] Oct. 7, 2005. Accessed Dec. 8, 2006 <http://www.globalresearch.ca/index.php context=viewArticle&code=HAS20051007&articleId=1054.>

_____. "Iraqi Women Under US Occupation." Global Research [online posting], May 6, 2005. Accessed Dec. 8, 2006 <http:/www.globalresearch.ca/index.phpcontext =viewArticle&code=HAS20050506&articleId=158.>

Hauerwas, Stanley. *Christian Existence Today: Essays on Church, World, and Living in Between.* Durham, NC: Labyrinth, 1998.

_____. *A Community of Character: Towards a Constructive Christian Social Ethic.* Notre Dame: University of Notre Dame Press, 1981.

_____. *Dispatches from the Front.* Durham, NC: Duke University Press, 1994.

_____. "On Being a Christian and an American." *A Better Hope.* Grand Rapids: Brazos Press, 2002: 29-44.

_____. "Preaching as Though We Had Enemies." In Brad J. Kallenberg. *Ethics as Grammar: Changing the Postmodern Subject.* Notre Dame: University of Notre Dame Press, 2001: 139.

Hedges, Chris. *American Fascists: the Christian Right and the War on America.* Parsippany, NJ: Free Press, 2007.

Heinrich, Clark. *Strange Fruit: Alchemy, Religion and Magical Foods: A Speculative History.* London: Bloomsbury, 1995.

Hinkelammert, Franz J. "Changes in the Relationships Between Third World Countries and First World Countries." *Spirituality of the Third World,* eds. K.C. Abraham and Bernadette Mbuy-Beya. Maryknoll, NY: Orbis, 1994: 10-32.

_____. *Cultura de la Esparanza y Sociedad sin Exclusion.* San Jose: DEI, 1995.

Horsley, Richard A. *Jesus and Empire: The Kingdom of God and the New World Disorder.* Minneapolis: Augsburg Fortress, 2002.

_____, and Neil Asher Silberman, *The Message and the Kingdom: How Jesus and Paul Ignited a Revolution and Changed the Ancient World.* Minneapolis: Augsburg Fortress, 2002.

Howard, Robert. "Is America Babylon?" *Wake up, America* [online posting]. Accessed December 7, 2005 <http:// www.theforbiddenknowledge.com/hardtruth/ america_babylon.>

Irenaeus. "Against Heresies." *Ante Nicene Fathers, Volume 1: Apostolic Fathers*, ed. Alexander Roberts. Grand Rapids: Eerdmans, 1988.

Janssen, Diederik F. "Become Big and I'll Give You Something to Eat: Thoughts and Notes on Boyhood Sexual Health." Unedited draft of in press article (2005). Accessed May 6, 2006 <http://www2.rz.huberlin.de/sexology/ GESUND/ARCHIV/GUS/JANSSEN 2005D.HTM.>

Johnson-Hill, Jack A. *I-Sight: The World of Rastafari: An Interpretive Sociological Account of Rastafarian Ethics*. London: The Scarecrow Press, 1995.

Jowett, Benjamin. "On the Interpretation of Scripture." *Essays and Reviews, 7th ed*. London: Green, Longman and Roberts, 1861: 378-395.

Kellermann, Bill Wylie, ed. *A Keeper of the Word: Selected Writings of William Stringfellow*. Grand Rapids: Wm. B. Eerdmans, 1994.

Kovacs, Judith and Christopher Rowland. *Revelation: The Apocalypse of Jesus Christ*. Oxford: Blackwell Publishing, 2004.

Krauthamer, Christian J. "The Emanuel-Fuchs Voucher Plan for Health System Reform." *American Medical Association Journal of Ethics*, July 2005. Accessed Oct. 17, 2006 <https://journalofethics.ama-assn.org/article/emanuel-fuchs-voucher-plan-health-system-reform/2005-07.>

Kuhn, David Paul and Ben Smith. "Messianic rhetoric infuses Obama rallies." *Politico*, Dec. 9, 2007.

Kwok, Pui-lan. *Postcolonial Imagination and Feminist Theology*. Louisville, KY: Westminster John Knox, 2005.

Landes, Richard. "Apocalypse: A Roundtable Discussion." *Frontline*, Sept. 1999. Accessed Feb. 1, 2007 <http://www.pbs.org/wgbh/pages/frontline/shows/apocalypse/roundtable/tres.html.>

Leclercq, Jean. *Monks and Love in Twelfth Century France*. Oxford: Clarendon, 1979.

Lewis, C.S. "The World's Last Night." *The Essential C.S. Lewis*. New York: Simon and Schuster, 1996: 385-414.

Lindsey, Hal. *The Everlasting Hatred: The Roots of Jihad*. Murietta, CA: Oracle House, 2002.

_____. *The Late Great Planet Earth*. Grand Rapids: Zondervan, 1998.

Lorber, Judith. *Breaking the Bowls: Degendering and Feminist Change*. New York: W.W. Norton, 2005.

Lusetich, Robert. "Climate science was doctored." *The Australian*, March 21, 2007.

MacIntyre, Alasdair. *Marxism and Christianity*. London: Duckworth, 1995.

Marley, Bob and the Wailers. "Babylon System." *Survival*, Island (1979) B00005MKA3.

Mathewes-Green, Frederica. "Bodies of Evidence." *Touchstone*, June 2005. Accessed March 12, 2006 <http://www.touchstonemag.com/archives/article.php id=18-05-027-f.>

McClendan, James. *Systematic Theology: Ethics I*. Nashville: Abingdon Press, 1986.

McLanahan, Sarah and Gary Sandefur. *Growing Up With a Single Parent: What Hurts, What Helps*. Cambridge: Harvard University Press, 2006.

Miller, Mark Crispin. "Big Media." *The Nation*, Jan. 7, 2002: 40-51.

Mounce, Robert. *The Book of Revelation*. Grand Rapids, MI: Eerdmans, 1977.

Murphy, Frederick J. *Fallen is Babylon: The Revelation to John*. Harrisburg, PA: Trinity Press International, 1998.

Naked. Dir. Mike Leigh. Thin Man, 1993. Film.

Neuhaus, Richard John. "Our American Babylon." *First Things* 158, Dec. 2005: 23-28.

"The New Face of Iraq" [online posting]. Accessed Mar. 29, 2007 < http://www.mnf -iraq.com/index.phpoption=com_content&task=view&id=16&Itemid=5.>

Newman, John Henry. "The Patristical Idea of Antichrist in Four Lectures." *The Rule of Our Warfare: John Henry Newman and the True Christian Life*, ed. John Hulsman. New York: Scepter, 2003: 176-207.

Nye, Jr., Joseph F. "What New World Order?" *Foreign Affairs*. March 1, 1992.

Ogletree, Thomas. *The World Calling: the Church's Witness in Politics and Society*. Louisville: WJK Press, 2004.

Olds, Sharon. "No Thanks, Mrs. Bush." *The Nation*, Oct. 10, 2005: 5.

Orwell, George. *1984*. New York: Signet Books, 1961.

"President Bush the Devil? Asks National Association of Evangelicals." *Christian Newswire*, Sept. 21, 2006.

"President Hugo Chavez Delivers Remarks at the U.N. General Assembly." *Washington Post*, Sept. 20, 2006.

Rabinow, Paul. *The Foucault Reader*. New York: Pantheon, 1984.

Rauschenbusch, Walter. *A Theology for the Social Gospel*. Nashville: Abingdon Press, 1990.

"Recommendations for Policies and Programs," *Abortion in Women's Lives*, eds. Heather D. Boonstra, Rachel Benson Gold, Cory L. Richards, Lawrence B. Finer. New York: Guttmacher Institute, May 4, 2006. Accessed Oct. 7, 2006 <https://www.guttmacher.org/sites/default/files/pdfs/pubs/2006/05/04/AiWL.pdf>.

Reno, R.R. "Stanley Hauerwas," *Blackwell Companion to Political Theology*, eds. Peter Scott and William T. Cavanaugh. Malden, MA: Blackwell, 2003: 309-321.

Rosenberg, Joel. Interview by Kyra Phillips. *Live from CNN*, July 26, 2006 - 15:00 ET. Accessed Nov. 8, 2006 <http://transcripts.cnn.com/TRANSCRIPTS/0607/26/lol.05.html.>

Roy, Arundhati. *War Talk*. Cambridge: South End Press, 2003.

Rueda, Jorge. "Chavez deepens Petrocaribe oil pledges." *Business Week*, Aug. 11, 2007. Accessed Aug. 11, 2007 <http://www.businessweek.com/ap/financialnews/D8QV4RUG1.htm.>

Russell, Bertrand. "Impact of Science on Society." London: Routledge, 1985.

Sack, Ronald H. "Nebuchadnezzar." *Anchor Bible Dictionary* (IV): 1059.

Sahagun, Louis. "End Times Groups Want Apocalypse Soon." *Los Angeles Times*, Jun. 22, 2006.

Said, Edward. "Preface to Orientalism." *Al-Ahram*, Aug. 2003: 7-13.

Sardar, Ziauddin, and Merryl Wyn Davies. *Why Do People Hate America?* New York: Disinformation Co., 2002.

Schaef, Finley. "Venezuela's Pres. Chavez Speaks at SPSAW." *Memorial UMC Newsletter*, Vol. 10 No. 9, October 2005. Accessed April 6, 2007 <http://www.gbgm-umc.org/memorialny/news100105.html.>

Schussler Fiorenza, Elisabeth. *The Book of Revelation: Justice and Judgment*. Philadelphia: Fortress, 1985.

_____. *Revelation: Vision of a Just World*. Minneapolis: Fortress, 1991.

Sider, Ronald J. *Rich Christians in an Age of Hunger*. Dallas: Word Publishing, 1990.

Smallwood, E. Mary. *Josephus: The Jewish War*, trans. G.A. Williamson. London: Penguin, 1981.

Soble, Alan. "Philosophy, Medicine, and Healthy Sexuality." *Sexuality and Medicine, Vol.1*, ed. Earl E. Shelp. Boston: D. Reidel Publishing Company, 1987.

Solomon, Robert C. "Heterosex." *Sexuality and Medicine, Vol.1,* ed. Earl E. Shelp. Boston: D. Reidel Publishing Company, 1987.

Stackhouse, Max. "Public Theology and Democratic Society." *The Church's Public Role: Retrospect and Prospect,* ed. Dieter T. Hessel. Grand Rapids: Eerdmans, 1993: 65-85.

Stringfellow, William. *An Ethic for Christians and Other Aliens in a Strange Land.* Eugene, OR: Wipf and Stock Publishers, 2004.

_____. *A Private and Public Faith.* Eugene, OR: Wipf and Stock, 1999.

Susskind, Yifat. "Promising Democracy, Imposing Theocracy: Gender-Based Violence and the US War on Iraq." *MADRE* [online posting] March 6, 2007. Accessed March 9, 2007 <http://www.madre.org/articles/me/iraqreport.html.>

Tavernese, Sabrina and Donald G. McNeil, Jr. "Iraqi Dead May Total 600,000, Study Says." *New York Times,* Oct. 11, 2006.

TeSelle, Eugene. "How Do We Recognize a Status Confessionis?" *Theology Today,* April 1988.

The Third Book of Hermas, or *Similitudes* [online posting]. Accessed Mar. 1, 2007 <http://www.earlychristianwritings.com/shepherd.html.>

Thoreau, Henry David. "Civil Disobedience." *The Portable Thoreau*, ed. Carl Bode. New York: Penguin, 194

Turkle, Sherry. *Life on the Screen: Identity in the Age of the Internet*. New York: Simon and Schuster, 1995.

Unger, Craig. "American Rapture." *Vanity Fair*, Dec. 2005. Accessed Apr. 3, 2007 <http://www.vanityfair.com/politics/features/2005/12/rapture200512.>

Volf, Miroslav. "Liberation Theology after the End of History: An Exchange/Against a Pretentious Church: A Rejoinder to Bell's Response," in *Modern Theology* 19:2, April 2003: 268-281.

Wainwright, Arthur W. *Mysterious Apocalypse*. Nashville: Abingdon, 1993.

Walker, Williston. *A History of the Christian Church*. New York: Scribner, 1985.

Watson, Duane. "Babylon." *Anchor Bible Dictionary* (I): 563.

Werpehowski, William. "Reinhold Niebuhr." *Blackwell Companion to Political Theology*, eds. Peter Scott and William T. Cavanaugh. Malden, MA: Blackwell, 2004: 192-207.

White, Ellen G. *The Great Controversy Between Christ and Satan*. Altamont, TN: Harvest, 1888.

Wilmer, Haddon. "Karl Barth." *The Blackwell Companion to Political Theology*, eds. Peter Scott and William T. Cavanaugh. Malden, MA: Blackwell, 2004: 131-148.

Wink, Walter. "Apocalypse Now?" *Christian Century*, Oct. 17, 2001: 16-19.

_____. *The Powers That Be: Theology for a New Millennium*. New York: Doubleday, 1998.

Yankelovitch, Daniel. *New Rules: Searching for Self-Fulfillment in a World Turned Upside Down*. New York: Random House, 1981.

Yoder, John Howard. *For the Nations*. Grand Rapids: Eerdmans, 1997.

_____. *The Politics of Jesus*. Grand Rapids: Eerdmans, 1972.

_____. *The Royal Priesthood*, ed. M.G. Cartwright. Grand Rapids: Eerdmanns, 1994.

Zillman, Dolf and Jennings Bryant. "Pornography, Sexual Callousness, and the Trivialization of Rape." *Journal of Communications 32* (1982): 5-37.

"Zionists 'incarnation of Satan,' says Ahmadinejad." *Middle East Times*, March 1, 2007.

About the Author

Canaan Harris never gave much thought to the
Apocalypse until he had a vision of the Rapture
in his twenties and discovered he was in danger
of being left behind. Afterwards he felt called to
make a formal study of the Book of Revelation
and over the past 20 years he's devoted his life's
work to sharing the message of Christ's return.
Canaan is the Senior Pastor of Central Christian
Church in Denver, Colorado, where he has served
since 2007. He is married to Niki Jorgenson, and
they have two children, Ezekiel and Eden.